Dedication

This book is dedicated to the members of the Sierra Club, Greenpeace, the Audubon Society, and to those who seek to live in harmony with our fellow creatures.

"Cooling it" on the trail

HIKING KAUAI

The Garden Isle

By Robert Smith

A Hawaiian Outdoor Adventures Publication

First edition 1977
Second edition 1979
Third edition 1983
Fourth printing March, 1987
Fourth edition 1989

Copyright ©1977,1979,1983,1989 by Robert Smith

Maps by Kevin G. Chard

All photos by Robert Smith

Library of Congress Card Catalog 83-60684

Int'l Standard Book Number 0-924308-00-1

Manufactured in the United States

Published by
Hawaiian Outdoor Adventures Publications
P.O. Box 30697
Long Beach, CA 90853

Acknowledgements

I am indebted to a number of people who generously offered their time and effort to make this book possible. Ralph E. Daehler, District Forester for the State of Hawaii and Mac Hori, Park Supervisor at Kokee State Park, contributed their knowledge and the resources of their respective departments. I am particularly grateful for their patience and good humor in response to my queries and requests. A very special "mahalo" to Roy Fujioka for sharing his knowledge of the island and to Carol, Francis and Mac Fujioka for their generosity.

       — Robert Smith
          Long Beach, CA
          January, 1989

Books by Robert Smith

Hawaii's Best Hiking Trails

Hiking Maui, the Valley Isle

Hiking Oahu, the Capital Isle

Hiking Hawaii, the Big Island

Hiking Kauai, the Garden Isle

Contents

Waimea Canyon

Part I: Introduction

Kauai

Na Pali Coast

Kalalau Tr.

Lumahai Bch. Tr. [2]

Haena

Haena

Hanalei

Kilauea

Hologa Bch. Tr. [4]

56

Hanalei River/ Okolehau Trails [3]

Keahua Trails [6]

Kapaa

Nonou Mountain Trails

5

Lydgate Park

Lydgate Park Tr. [7]

56

Kapaia

57

51

Wailua Falls Tr. [8]

Mt. Waialeale Elev. 5080

Kilohana Crater Tr.

9

50

Puhi

Paipu Bch. Petroglyphs Tr.

Poipu [10]

Kokee St. Pk./ Waimea Canyon Trails [14]

Lawai

530

Koloa

520

Kalaheo

Kokuiolono Park Tr. [11]

54

Polihale St. Pk. Tr. [13]

55

Hanapepe

Waimea Tr. [12]

550

Waimea

Mana

50

Waimea

Trails □
Highways —O—

The Island

Kauai offers more natural beauty than most people can absorb. Island trails lead to magnificent waterfalls, to breathtaking vistas into Kauai's canyonlands and to the wilderness area along the Na Pali Coast. No one I have ever known has been disappointed by this enchanted land.

It is important to remember, however, that natural and man-made forces have had and continue to have a dramatic impact on Hawaii's topography. Periodic volcanic eruptions, 400-plus inches of rain in several places, earthquakes, the influx of new residents, and the increasing numbers of visitors affect trail conditions. A trail that was cleared and brushed and in good condition can become overgrown after a few weeks of heavy rain, particularly if it is not heavily traveled. For example, the trails in the Kokee/Waimea area were in very good condition in the summer of 1988. However, 200-500 inches of rain annually in that area impacts greatly on trail conditions so that the description in this book may differ a bit from what you experience.

In addition to damage to trails caused by natural forces, some people destroy or remove trailhead signs, trail markers and trail mileage posts for some inexplicable reason. Consequently, I have provided clear directions to trailheads and a trail description that does not rely on posted trail markers.

Some people call it Kauai-a-mano-ka-lani-po —
"The fountainhead of many waters from on high and
bubbling up from below." Others regard it as "The
Grand Canyon of the Pacific" or "The Garden Island"
and still others say it is "The land of the Menehune."
But even if you just call it "Kauai" — time of plenty,
or fruitful season — it is still a land of beauty, grandeur
and adventure, and a challenge to the outdoorsperson.
There is a lot of hiking pleasure packed into this almost
circular little island of 555 square miles.

Kauai lays claim to a number of firsts and unique
characteristics. It is the oldest island in the Hawaiian
Islands, it is the northern-most inhabited island in the
chain, and it was the first one visited by Captain Cook
— though that is a rather dubious distinction. Still
other things of local pride include Mt. Waialeale, the
wettest spot on earth; the only place on earth where the
iliau, a rare and unique plant, is to be found; and the
home of the legendary Menehune, a race of pygmies
who were short, industrious, strong, and highly skilled
workers in stone.

Not unlike the neighboring islands, tourism on
Kauai with its 47,000 inhabitants has grown to the
point that over 1,000,000 people annually visit it.
Kauai lies 102 air miles northwest of Honolulu —
about a 20-minute flight. Most visitors to Kauai are
seeking its solitude and slower pace of life, and many
find these in the verdant valleys of the romote Na Pali
coast and in the lush canyon lands of Waimea. Con-
veniently, the State of Hawaii and the County of Kauai
have established miles of trails and jeep roads into
remote areas which will reveal some of the island's
secrets.

Using This Book

With few exceptions, hiking on Kauai does not require any special equipment or skill. Many places are readily accessible even to the tenderfoot and to people not inclined to hike much. The hikes included in this guide are in four categories, and a glace at the Hiking Chart below will enable you to make a decision based on your interests, your skill, and the time you wish to devote to your hike. The "Family Hikes" are short, easy strolls for people with small children and people who are unaccustomed to strenuous activity. Hikes in the "Hardy Family" category require some effort, and sound physical condition. Hikes in the "Strenuous" and the "Difficult" classifications are more serious hikes, and require not only sound physical condition but also good footwear and sometimes additional equipment. Most of them are full-day or overnight hikes.

The Hiking Chart provides the information necessary for a person to choose a hike. It includes one-way trail time and distance, elevation gain, if any, and equipment needed. Obviously, trail time depends on your pace and physical condition, and the time you devote to sightseeing or swimming. The time given is based on a leisurely pace, including time to picnic, to swim and to explore.

The trail rating in the Hiking Chart is based on whether there is a trail that is either maintained or sufficiently traveled so that it is distinguishable. However, do not be discouraged by a "rough" or "no trail" rating, for in many cases a stream or some readily identifiable physical characteristic marks the way.

Driving time and mileage are based on the posted speed limit and are measured from Lihue, the center of tourist activity and the county seat. (The islands of Kauai and Niihau makeup Kauai County.) Specific

Hiking Chart

Hiking Area Number		Hike Rating				Trail Time (one-way)			Trail Rating			From Lihue		Equipment					Features				
		Family	Hardy family	Strenuous	Difficult	Distance (miles)	Time (hours)	Gain (feet)	Good trail	Rough trail	No trail	Miles	Time (hours)	Raingear	Boots recommended	Tennis Shoes O.K.	Carry Water	Take Food	Swimming	Waterfalls	Views	Historical Sites	Fruits
1	Kalalau Trail											38	1										
	to Hanakapiai		X			2	1		X					X	X	X	X		X		X		X
	to Hanakapiai Falls			X		2	1½			X				X	X	X	X	X	X	X		X	X
	To Hanakoa			X		4	2½		X					X	X		X	X	X	X	X	X	X
	to Hanakoa Falls	(Side Trail)				.4	1/4			X				X	X	X			X	X			X
	To Kalalau Beach				X	4.8	3		X					X	X		X	X	X	X	X	X	X
2	Lumahai Beach	X				.2	1/6		X			33	3/4			X			X		X		
3	Hanalei River		X			2	1			X		31	3/4			X	X	X	X		X		
	Okolehau Trail			X		2.25	2	1272	X			29.9	3/4	X	X		X	X			X	X	X
4	Moloaa Beach	X				1.5	1		X			18	1/2	X		X	X	X	X		X		X
5	Nonou Mountain																						
	Eastside			X		2	1½	1250	X			7	1/4	X	X	X	X	X			X		X
	Westside			X		1.5	1	1000	X			10	1/2	X	X	X	X	X			X		X
6	Keahua Trails																						
	Keahua Arboretum	X				.5	1/2		X			12	1/2	X		X	X		X				
	Moalepe Tr.			X		2.5	1½	500	X			12	1/2	X	X	X	X				X		X
	Kuilau Ridge Tr.			X		2.1	1½		X			12	1/2	X	X	X	X				X		X
7	Lydgate Park	X				1	1		X			6	1/4			X			X		X	X	X
8	Wailua Falls				X	.5	1/2				X	5	1/3	X	X				X	X	X	X	X
9	Kilohana Crater			X		2.5	1½	1000	X			4	1/4	X			X	X			X	X	X
10	Poipu Beach Petroglyphs	X				1	1/2				X	14	1/2	X	X	X			X			X	
11	Kukuiolono Park	X				.5	1/2				X	12	1/2			X					X	X	
12	Waimea (Russian Fort)	X				.5	1/2		X			22	3/4			X			X		X	X	
13	Polihale State Park			X		3	1½				X	38	1			X	X	X	X		X	X	
14	Kokee/Waimea Canyon											38	1½										
	Southeast																						
	Black Pipe Tr.			X		.4	1/2		X					X	X	X	X	X			X		
	Canyon Tr.				X	1.7	2	800	X					X	X		X	X	X	X	X		
	Cliff Tr.	X				.1	1/6		X					X	X	X					X		
	Ditch Tr.			X		3.5	4		X					X	X		X	X			X		X
	Halemanu-Kokee Tr.	X				1.2	1		X					X	X	X	X	X					X
	Iliau Nature Loop Tr.	X				.3	1/4		X							X					X	X	
	Kaluahaulu-Waialae Tr.				X	7	FD*			X				X	X		X	X	X	X	X		
	Kaluapuhi Tr.	X				1	1		X					X	X	X	X	X					X
	Koaie Canyon Tr.			X		3	2			X				X	X		X	X	X	X	X	X	X
	Kukui Tr.			X		2.5	2	2000	X					X	X		X	X	X	X	X		X
	Kumuwela Tr.	X				.8	1	300	X					X	X	X	X	X					
	Puu Ka Ohelo/Berry Flat Trail	X				2	1½		X					X	X	X	X						X
	Waialae Canyon Tr.	(In Canyon)				.3	1/2			X				X	X		X	X	X		X		
	Waimea Canyon Tr.	(In Canyon)				1.5	2		X					X	X		X	X	X	X	X		
	Waininiua Tr.	X				.6	1/2		X					X	X	X	X	X					
	Northwest																						
	Alakai Swamp Tr.			X		3.5	3			X				X	X		X	X			X		
	Awaawapuhi Tr.			X		3.1	3		X					X	X		X	X			X		
	Honopu Tr.			X		2.5	2½			X				X	X		X	X			X		
	Kawaikoi Stream Tr.	X				1.3	3/4		X					X	X	X	X	X					X
	Kohua Ridge Tr.			X		2.5	3		X					X	X	X	X	X			X		
	Mohihi-Waialae Tr.				X	9	FD*			X				X	X		X	X			X		
	Nualolo Tr.			X		3.8	3	1500	X					X	X		X	X			X		X
	Naulolo Cliff Tr.	(Side Trail)				2.1	1½		X					X	X		X	X			X		X
	Pihea Tr.			X		3.75	3		X					X	X		X	X			X		
	Poomau Canyon Tr.	X				.3	1/4		X					X	X	X	X		X	X			
	Mt. Waialeale Tr.				X	6	FD*	1500		X				X	X		X	X			X	X	X

*Full-day hike

driving instructions for each hike appear with that hike. There is no public transportation on the island. At present, hitchhiking is allowed. If you hitchhike, be patient, for rides are hard to come by in the outlying areas.

For most hikes your only needs are food, water, a first-aid kit, and sound footwear. Although hiking boots are not essential on most hikes, I wear them because I am particularly fond of my feet, and I recommend them. Water is available from streams in many areas, but should be boiled, treated or filtered before drinking. Cattle, pigs and goats usually share the stream water with you. I suggest you begin each hike with one quart of water per person. Due to the heavy rainfall on Kauai, dry firewood is rare, so a small, light, reliable backpacking stove is a convenience and a comfort. A hot cup of tea, coffee or soup is invigorating while waiting out a passing storm, and a hot breakfast is desireable after a wet night. Lastly, most hikers find shorts adequate on most trails. However, along the Kalalau Trail some people shed all clothing for either physical or psychological reasons — I have not decided which.

In the text preceding a trail description is a map to help you get to the trailhead. These maps are not exactly to scale but are drawn to emphasize important features. For each hike, I give the hike's features as well as camping information (where applicable), one-way hiking distance and time (unless otherwise noted), driving instructions, special instructions, and introductory notes about the hike.

In the trail description, I usually mention the flora and fauna along the trail, particularly the unusual and the unique, in hopes of adding to your hiking enjoyment. But I mention only a few examples, and you may wish to buy one or several small guides to plants and animals common to the islands. These are available at bookstores on the island.

Camping

Camping out on Kauai will add another dimension to your visit. Campgrounds on Kauai range from adequate to good, contain most of the amenities, and are either free or inexpensive. The accompanying map locates and cites the facilities available at state and county campgrounds. A third jurisdiction, the Division of Forestry, also provides a number of campgrounds, camping shelters, and camping areas, which are noted on individual maps throughout the book. A word about each kind of campground should be helpful.

First, the Hawaii state parks at Kokee and Polihale offer excellent facilities and are free. Camping is limited to five days per 30-day period for each campground, and is by permit only, obtained through the Department of Land & Natural Resources, Division of State Parks, Room 306, in the State Building in Lihue (3060 Eiwa St.); or if you choose to write for a permit, write to P.O. Box 1671, Lihue, Kauai, Hawaii, 96766. The Division of State Parks also regulates camping and hiking along the Na Pali Coast: Hanakapiai, Hanakoa, Kalalau — the three major valleys along the wilderness trail. Camping permits are required and may be obtained from the Division of State Parks (address above). Camping is limited to five nights total along the Na Pali Coast in any 30-day period. Hanakapiai and Hanakoa are limited to one night each in that period. Hiking permits are required beyond Hanakapiai Valley, even for day hiking. When writing for reservations for all of the state parks, include the dates desired, the park, the number of persons and their names. The state cabins at Kokee are operated by a concessionaire (see Hiking Area No. 14 for details and reservation information).

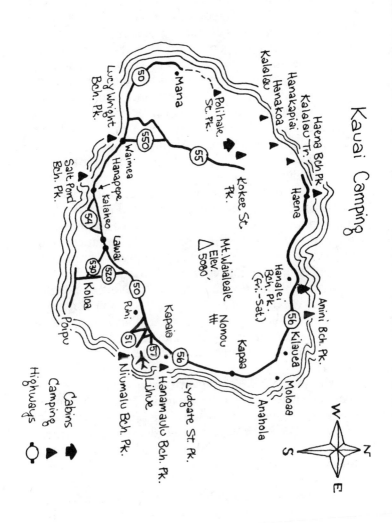

Kauai Camping

Secondly, the County of Kauai has numerous compgrounds and beach parks around the island. County camping costs $3 per adult per day (Hawaii residents are free). Persons under 18 are free if accompanied by an adult. Permits are not issued to persons under 18. Camping permits are issued for up to seven days at each campsite. A total of sixty (60) camping days per year is allowed. For reservations, write Department of Parks and Recreation, County of Kauai, 4280A Rice St., Building B, Lihue, Hawaii, 96766. Include your name, address, campground desired, dates, and the number of persons in your party, with names and ages. DO NOT forward fees. Payment and permit must be issued in person at the office (M-F, 7:45-4:30) or after hours nearby at the police station.

Last, the Hawaii State Division of Forestry maintains a number of trailside camping areas in the forest reserve, which are identified on the individual maps preceding the text of each hiking area. Camping is limited to three nights within a 30-day period, but this regulation is not regularly enforced. Neither permits nor reservations are necessary. Registration is by sign-in at the trailhead upon entering and leaving a forest-reserve area. All the facilities are primitive and lacking in amenities, but to some people that is their best feature.

Campers are well advised to bring their own equipment because locally it is expensive. For rentals on the island, I recommend Hanalei Camping & Backpacking with a store in Hanalei and Kekaha. Their stores are well-stocked with rentals and a complete line of hiking and backpacking needs, and their staff is well-informed and helpful.

Camping in Hawaii has always been an enjoyable and inexpensive way to experience the Islands. Recently, however, some campers have been beaten and a few have been killed. Most of the beatings have been committed by local men, according to the victims. Most of the assaults have taken place at campgrounds that were close to cities or towns where locals congregate. There has been little or no problem in remote and wilderness areas or in the national parks. The best advice is to avoid camping in areas readily accessible to locals and to avoid contact with groups of people. I recommend Kokee State Park, Haena Beach Park and Salt Pond Beach Park. The latter is one of the best beach camping places in Hawaii.

Camping at Salt Pond

Food and Equipment

Although food is more expensive on Kauai than on the mainland, it is readily available in most of the towns. You may visit a local delicatessen that prepares box lunches containing local favorites such as tempura, sweet-and-sour spare ribs and sushi. When fruits are not available along the trail, be certain to visit a local market or roadside stand for mango, papaya, pineapple, passion fruit, and local avocado which comes in the large economy size.

The short-term visitor and the casual hiker do not need a lot of sophisticated hiking equipment. For a day hike, the following equipment is recommended.

Daypack
Hiking boots or tennis shoes
Plastic water bottle, quart size
Swiss Army knife
Insect repellent
Shorts
Bathing suit
Sun screen and tanning lotion
Sun glasses
Whistle for each child
Camera and film
Poncho or raingear
Hat or sun visor
Towel
Waterproof matches
Hiking Kauai — The Garden Isle

Although the backpacker or overnight hiker visiting the island may have had previous experience, here are some items of equipment and some tips that should prove helpful.

Pick your own

BACKPACK CHECKLIST

  <u>General Equipment:</u>
   Frame and pack
   Lightweight sleeping bag or blanket (beach camping)
   Sleeping bag (over 4,000 feet)
   Backpack tent with rainfly
   Plastic ground cover
   Sleep pad
   Plastic bottle, quart size
   Swiss Army knife
   Flashlight
   40 feet of nylon cord
   First-aid kit

  <u>Cooking Gear:</u>
   Backpack stove
   Fuel
   Cooking pots
   Sierra cup
   Fork, spoon
   Plastic bowl
   Waterproof matches

  <u>Clothing:</u>
   Poncho or raingear
   Pants, shorts or bathing suit
   Hat
   Bandana (doubles as washcloth)
   Underwear
   Socks
   Hiking boots

Toilet Articles:
   Soap (biodegradable)
   Toothbrush/powder-paste
   Part-roll of toilet paper
   Chapstick
   Comb
   Mirror
   Insect repellent
   Sunscreen and tanning lotion

Miscellaneous:
   Sun glasses
   Camera/film
   Plastic bags
   Fishing gear

   Hiking and backpacking are pleasurable when the hiker has taken the time to plan his trip and to prepare his equipment.

Camping at Kokee State Park

Hawaiian Made Easy

For your interest, throughout the text wherever a Hawaiian place name is used, I have provided a literal translation if possible. In many instances, Hawaiian names have multiple meanings and even the experts sometimes disagree over the literal meaning. The meanings given here are based on the best information available and on the context in which the name is used. As students of the environment, the Hawaiians had a flair for finding the most expressive words to describe their physical surroundings.

Many visitors are reluctant to try to pronounce Hawaiian words. But with a little practice and a knowledge of some simple rules, you can develop some language skill and add to your Hawaiian experience. Linguists regard Hawaiian as one of the most fluid and melodious languages of the world. There are only 12 letters in the Hawaiian alphabet: five vowels, a,e,i,o,u, and seven consonants, h,k,l,m,n,p,w. Hawaiian is spelled phonetically. Correct pronunciation is easy if you do not try to force English pronunciation onto the Hawaiian language. Vowel sounds are simple: a=ah; e=eh; i=ee; o=oh; and u=oo. Consonant sounds are the same as in English with the exception of w. Rules for w are not adhered to with any consistency by local people. Generally, w is pronounced "w" at the beginning of a word and after a. For example. Waimea is pronounced "Wai-may-ah" and wala-wala is "Wah-lah-wah-lah." Hawaiians also usually pronounce w as "w" when it follows o or u; auwaha is "ah-oo-wah-hah," and hoowali is "hoh-oh-wah-lee." When w is next to the final letter of a word, it is variably pronounced "w" and "v"; Wahiawa is "wah-he-ah-wa," but Hawi is "ha-vee." Listen to the locals for their treatment of this sound. Since the Hawaiian language is not strongly accented, the visitor will probably be understood without employing any accent.

Part II:
Hiking Trails on Kauai

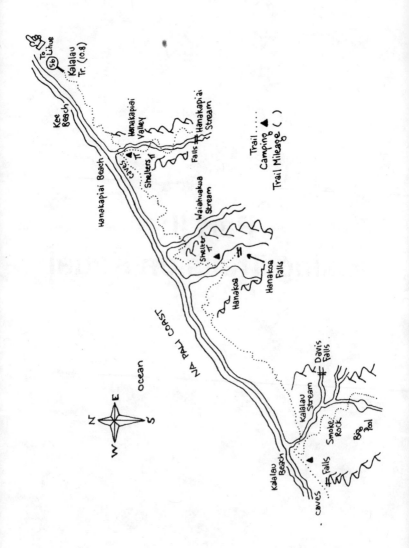

Kalalau Trail
(Hiking Area No. 1)

Rating: See individual hikes.

Features: Wilderness area, camping, coastal views, fruits, waterfalls, swimming, historical sites.

Permission: Camping permits are required for Hanakapiai, Hanakoa and Kalalau valleys. Permits for camping must be obtained from the Division of State Parks (see Camping section in the INTRODUCTION for details and Appendix for addresses).

Hiking Distance & Time: See individual hikes.

Driving Instructions: 38 miles, 1 hour from Lihue. North on Route 56 to road's end.

Introductory Notes: When people talk about hiking on Kauai, they talk about visiting the uninhabited valleys of the Na Pali (the cliffs) Coast as evidenced by the comments registered by hikers on the sign-in at the trailhead. "Fantastic," "incredible," "paradise," "The most beautiful place in the world," are just a few of the expressions noted. Kalalau ("the straying") trail to the end of the beach (10.8 miles) is the most exciting hike on the island.

Few who have hiked the Kalalau Trail will deny its grandeur and its captivating allure. Cliffs rise precipitously above the blue-green water and the rugged, rocky north shore of Kauai. The valleys of the Na Pali Coast are accessible only by foot or by boat, and only during the summer when the tides expose a generous sandy beach, which is ripped away each year by winter storms. In the summer of 1988, the trail was in good condition.

Na Pali Coast

Hiking the entire trail to Kalalau requires back-packing equipment for a comfortable, safe trip. Sound hiking boots are essential, since a good deal of your hiking is alternately on soft cinders and ash and rocks along the precipitous coast and on rocky trails in the valleys. A strong, waterproof tent is needed to stand up under the wind at Kalalau and the rain at Hanakoa. Although fresh water is available all along the trail, you should boil the water or purify it or use a good filtration device; people, goats and pigs are using the same stream. A light sleeping bag or light blanket is adequate, particularly during the summer months when the nighttime temperature is very comfortable. Little clothing is necessary during the day, and it is still somewhat common to find both sexes hiking without any. A backpacking stove is recommended since dry firewood is difficult to find and tree cutting is not permitted.

The trailhead for the Kalalau Trail is at the end of the road, where you will find several parking areas. A word of caution, however, may save some grief: vehicles left overnight in the parking places are frequently vandalized so do not leave anything in your car. Furthermore, if rental car companies learn that you are backpacking they usually won't rent to you even if you have a reservation. Hitchhiking, which is legal on Kauai, is an alternative to renting a car. Taxi service is available from the Princeville Airport.

In recent years, several companies have offered a shuttle service via Zodiac boats between the Hanalei

Kee Beach

area and Kalalau Valley. In 1988, they charged $100 roundtrip per person including backpack or $55 for one-way service. Look in the tourist newspapers and brochures for current services and prices.

On the Trail: Kee Beach to Hanakapiai Beach, 2 miles, 1 hour (trail rating: hardy family).

The trek to Hanakapiai (lit., "bay sprinkling food") Beach is an honest hike; it is one steep mile up and one steep mile down from Kee (lit., "avoidance") Beach on a wide, maintained trail. This is a much frequented trail because tourist publications promise a verdant valley resplendent with native and introduced flora. No one is disappointed. Particularly abundant is the hala (Pandanus tectorius), an indigenous tree that grows in coastal areas. It is sometimes called "tourist pineapple," since the fruit resembles a pineapple and is jokingly identified as such by locals for tourists. Humor aside, the hala has been a valuable resource, the hollow trunk of the female tree being used as a pipe for drainage between taro patches. The leaves have commercial value being used for weaving many items such as baskets, mats and hats — hats being particularly popular with tourists. In the past, the fruit was eaten in times of famine and was used to make colorful necklaces. When the sections of the fruit were dried, they were used as brushes.

The first half mile up the cliff provides views at a couple of points back to Kee Beach and Haena ("wilderness") reefs. This part of the trail is usually shady because of the large trees and cool because of the trade winds and periodic rain showers. One source of shade is the large kukui (Aleurites moluccana) tree from which a beautiful and popular lei is made. To make a lei, each nut must be sanded, filed and polished to a brilliant luster that is acquired from its own oil.

Hanakapiai Beach

Until the advent of electricity, kukui-nut oil was burned for light. Nicknamed the "candlenut tree" its trunk was shaped into canoes by early Hawaiians.

The trail leads up and down from the 1/2 to the 1 1/4-mile marker. With any luck you may find some sweet guava (Psidium guajava), a small yellow, lemon-sized fruit that contains five times more vitamin C than an orange. Before eating one break it open and check for worms. They are tiny and are a little hard to see but are common in wild guava.

Near the 1-mile marker, look for a small springlet that flows year round and provides a welcomed face-splashing. At the 1 1/2-mile marker, you'll have your first view of Hanakapiai Beach below, with its generous beach (during the summer months) and its crashing surf. Look for wild orchids, with their delicate purplish flowers, thriving along the banks of the trail.

As you descend to the beach, several warning signs caution visitors not to swim in the ocean because of the heavy surf and of the presence of riptides and strong currents. Several drownings occur here in spite of the posted admonition. From across the stream, you can hike the trail into the valley and to the falls. I suggest a hike to the falls in the afternoon when it is more likely to be warm and sunny in the valley.

If you want to stay overnight at Hanakapiai Beach, you have a choice of campsites. There are numerous campsites on the west side of the stream beginning on the bluff overlooking the beach and extending into the valley. Some daring campers sleep in the cave located in the cliff that drops to the beach. It's too close to the ocean for me.

Hanakapiai Valley Trail, 2 miles, 1 1/2 hours (trail rating: strenuous).

The Hanakapiai Valley Trail follows the stream

and passes through a rain forest resplendent with native flora. The beginning of the trail on the west side of the valley contains some of the largest mango (Mangifera indica) trees anywhere. One grove surrounding the remains of a coffee mill contains a tree that is 23 feet in circumference. Obviously, it makes a shady sheltered campsite. The mango tree is not native to Hawaii, but its many varieties have done well there, and are popular with locals and tourists. However, the trees in this valley do not bear as well as those in drier areas because of a fungus that kills the blossoms in wet areas. Many people regard the mango fruit as second to none in taste and appearance.

The hike to the falls is a must not only because the falls are spectacular, but also because much serenity and enchantment are to be found in the valley. The first 1/4-mile is an easy trail that snakes along the stream. "Okolehau" ("okole" is translated "anus" or "buttocks"; and "hau" can mean "cool.") is the name of a Division of Forestry trail-crew shelter near the coffee mill which you may use when it is not occupied by a trail crew.

You will make three stream crossings. The trail is always easy to find because the valley is so narrow. However, be alert for unstable places caused by yearly heavy rains and flooding. The last 1/2-mile is the most difficult part, but perhaps the most enchanting, with inviting pools and water slides and verdant growth. The trail is cut along the walls of the canyon in a number of places. Caution is well-advised.

Although the pool at the base of the falls is inviting, caution is again advised for there is danger from falling rocks from the cliffs and the ledge above the falls. Hanakapiai Falls cascades and falls about 300 feet in the back of a natural amphitheater. You don't need to be told to swim and enjoy the pools and the

Hanakapiai Falls

surrounding area. You will find safe pools away from falling rocks.

Hanakapiai to Hanakoa, 4 miles, 2 1/2 hours (trail rating: strenuous).

Serious hiking on the trail to Kalalau begins at this point as the trail climbs out of Hanakapiai Valley on a series of switchbacks for one mile. This is the most difficult section of the entire 11-mile trek. Hiking here in the morning means that the sun will be at your back and, with the trade wind, it should be relatively cool. The trail does not drop to sea level again until Kalalau Beach, some nine miles along the cliffs.

There are two small valleys before Hanakoa. The first is Hoolulu (lit., "to lie in sheltered waters"), which is first viewed from a cut in the mountain at the 3 1/4-mile marker. From here you descend to cross the valley and climb the opposite side. Hoolulu is thickly foliated with native and introduced plants that are typical of most valleys on the island. Ti, guava, morning glory, mountain orchids, and different kinds of ferns can be identified along with the larger kukui, koa and hala trees. Be careful at points where the trail narrows along a precipitous slope.

Waiahuakua Valley, at the 4 1/4-mile marker, is broader than Hoolulu. In June-August, you are likely to find delicious ohia ai (Eugenia malaccensis), or mountain apples, growing along the trail. Abundant in Waiahuakua, these trees have smooth, dark green leaves and some attain a height of 50 feet. The fruit is a small red or pinkish apple with a thin, waxen skin, while the meat is flesh-white, crisp and juicy, with a large brown seed in the center — a very tasty repast for those lucky enough to find some. Additionally, the valley abounds in coffee, ti, guava, kukui, and mango.

Hanakapiai Beach

At the 5 3/4-mile marker, you will get your first view of Hanakoa (lit., "bay of koa trees or of warriors") Valley which is a broad-terraced valley that was once cultivated by Hawaiians. Many of the terraced areas provide relatively sheltered camping sites. In addition, "Mango Shelter" has a roof-and-table and "Hanakoa Shack," a short distance away, is a Division of Forestry trail-crew shelter that is open to hikers when not in use by crews. In 1988, the "shack" was so dilapidated that it was of little value as a shelter. Both are located along the trail a short distance into the valley. Camping in Hanakoa is quite an experience since it receives frequent rains, and as soon as you dry out, it rains again. However, the afternoon can be warm and sunny, just perfect for a swim in one of the

Mountain apples

many pools in the stream and a sunbath on the large, warm rocks along the bank. These are a favorite of nude sun worshippers.

To Hanakoa Falls, .4 mile, 1/4 hour.

The trail (posted in 1988) begins between the stream crossing and the 6 1/2-mile marker and passes a wilderness campsite and terraced areas once used by the Hawaiians for growing taro from which the staple food poi is produced. The falls cascade down the pali in a breathtaking setting. If you plan to camp in Hanakoa, you should be prepared for a lot of rain, wetness and humidity. To compensate, you will have solitude and a private swimming pool if you camp away from where the trail crosses the stream.

Hanakoa to Kalalau Beach, 4.8 miles, 3 hours (trail rating: strenuous).

Your physical condition and your hiking skill will be tested on this portion of the hike. Not only is most of the hiking on switchbacks that alternate up and down along a very precipitous cliff, but also the danger is increased by a number of slides along the trail. Another hazard is the hot afternoon sun unless you begin hiking early. However, the views of the northwest coastline are absolutely breathtaking and staggeringly beautiful. It is difficult to think of another view in the world that compares.

At the 6 1/2-mile marker, you enter land that until 1975 was part of the Makaweli (lit., "fearful features") cattle ranch owned by the Robinson Family who also own the island of Niihau off the coast of Kauai. The area becomes increasingly dry as you continue west, and only the smaller more arid types of vegetation survive, like sisal and lantana. Lantana (Lantana camara) is a popular flower that blossoms almost continuously. Its flowers vary in color from yellow to orange to pink to red; infrequently, they are white with a yellow center. If you hike in the early morning or late afternoon you're likely to frighten feral goats foraging near the trail and near some of the small streams along the trail.

Although there are only a few trail-milage markers over the rest of the route, there is no chance of getting lost. The trail is over open land and visible ahead. There are at least five reliable sources of water between Hanakoa and Kalalau. The admonition to treat, filter or to boil the water applies.

Pohakuao (lit., "day stone") is the last small valley before Kalalau. As you ascend the west side of Pohakuao along a pali with sparse foliage and reddish earth, you reach Red Hill, as it is known to locals, from which you get your first view of Kalalau, a welcome sight after a difficult three miles from Hanakoa. There is no mistaking Kalalau, for it is a large, broad valley some two miles wide and three miles long. From the ridge, a precipitous snake-like trail drops abruptly to Kalalau Stream where rushing water and cool pools await the weary hiker.

Camping is allowed only on the beach, in the trees fronting the beach and in the caves at the far end of the beach. Try to find a spot that will shelter you from the strong winds and the hot daytime sun. Some campers find shelter in the low scrub along the beach during the day and then sleep on the beach during the cool and usually wind-free nights. Lantana and common guava are particularly abundant along the trail in the beach area. You should easily find some ripe guava to add to your meals. Don't drink the stream water until you treat, filter or boil the water. The falls at the end of the beach by the caves is your best bet for safe water although you should treat, filter or boil the water also.

The water from the falls also serves the ferel goats that you will undoubtedly see in the morning and at dusk when they visit to refresh themselves. Most of the campers take a daily shower under the falls.

Kalalau abounds in a variety of life. Beach naupaka (Scaevola frutescens), with small, fragrant, white flowers, can be found near the beach, mixed with the low sisal and lantana. Hala, ti, ferns, bamboo, bananas, mango, kukui, monkeypod and many other species of flora can be identified. Rock terraces where Hawaiians planted taro as late as the 1920s are also common.

Some very daring people attempt to wade and swim around the point where the beach ends on the west side in an effort to visit Honopu (lit., "conch bay") Valley, the so-called "Valley of the Lost Tribe"

Kalalau Beach

— a reference to the legendary little people named Mu who once lived there. The swim around the point takes about 15 minutes but is very risky due to the strong current and undertow in the ocean. Occassionally, the tide is sufficiently low so that it is possible to walk to Honopu.

Locals and visitors enjoy speculating about the exploits and the hideouts of Kalalau's most famous citizen, Koolau. Commonly called "Koolau the Leper," this native Hawaiian was born in Kekaha in 1862. Three years after showing signs of leprosy, at the age of 27, Koolau and the other lepers of Kauai were ordered to the leper colony on Molokai, and were promised that their wives and children could accompany them. When the ship sailed without his wife and child, Koolau, realizing he had been tricked, dove overboard and swam ashore. Together with his wife and child he made the perilous descent into Kalalau Valley to join other lepers who sought to escape deportation. A year later, local authorities decided to round up the lepers, all of whom agreed to go to Molokai except Koolau. A sheriff's posse exchanged fire with Koolau, who shot and killed a deputy. Martial law was declared, and a detachment of the national guard was sent from Honolulu with orders to get their man dead or alive. A small cannon was mounted near the site where Koolau was thought to be hiding. In the ensuing "battle" Koolau shot two guardsmen and one accidentally shot and killed himself fleeing the leper. The remaining guardsmen fled from the valley to the beach. In the morning they blasted Koolau's hideout with their cannon. Believing him dead, the guardsmen left the valley. But Koolau had moved his family the night before the cannonading, and they lived in the valley for about five more years, always fearful that the guard was still looking for him. They hid during the

Na Pali Coast / Kalalau Valley

day and hunted for food at night. Tragically, their son developed signs of leprosy and soon died; a year later, the dread disease claimed Koolau. Piilani, his wife, buried her husband in the valley that had become their home along with his gun which had enabled them to be together to the end.

To some, Koolau is a folk hero who received unfair treatment by the government. Indeed, locals claim that Koolau frequently left his valley hideout to visit friends and relatives on Kauai. Whatever the facts, it makes for an interesting story and campfire conversation.

Kalalau Beach to Big Pool, 2 miles, 1 1/2 hour.
The trail into the valley begins on the west side of Kalalau Stream at the marked trailhead. Before heading into the valley, hike to the top of the knoll above the beach, also on the west side of the stream. The remains of a heiau — a pre-Christian place of worship — lie between the knoll and the beach and are clearly identifiable from this vantage point. Little is known about this nameless heiau. Remember that such places are still revered by many people, and a rock wrapped in a ti leaf and left on a heiau site is believed to protect the traveler.

From the trailhead, the trail parallels the stream for a short distance and then ascends an eroded rise. From here the trail alternately passes open and forested areas. In the wooded areas look for oranges, mango, common guava and rose apple. Each can be found in the valley and can supplement a backpackers diet. At the one-mile point, Smoke Rock is a convenient place to pause in an open area from which the entire valley can be viewed. This is the place where the valley marijuana growers and residents used to meet to smoke and to talk stories. The rest of the trail to Big Pool is under the shade of giant mango and rose apple trees. Before reaching Big Pool, a side stream crossing must be made. Heading into the valley, the next stream crossing is Kalalau Stream. Big Pool, a short distance from this crossing is easily identified. Two room-sized pools are separated by a natural water slide which is a joy to slip down into the cool water below. It's a delightful place to enjoy the sights and smells of Kalalau, Kauai's most precious treasure.

Playtime in Kalalau Valley

Lumahai Beach
(Hiking Area No. 2)

Rating: Family.

Features: Swimming, snorkeling, picnic, views.

Permission: None.

Hiking Distance & Time: .2 miles, 10 minutes.

Driving Instructions: 33 miles, 3/4 hour from Lihue. North on Route 56 past Hanalei, park by sign "Lumahai Beach."

Introductory Notes: Lumahai (lit., "a certain twist of the fingers in making string figures") Beach really doesn't qualify as a hike, but should be included in any visit to Kauai. Lumahai is regarded as the most beautiful beach on Kauai. It is certainly one of the most photographed, appearing in tourist papers and on calendars throughout the world. It has also appeared in many movies, most notable "South Pacific."

On the Trail: The Hawaiian Visitor's Bureau sign identifies the trail to the beach at a curve past the town

Lumahai Beach

of Hanalei. Park off the road and remove all valuables from your car. Unfortunately, even locked cars have not stopped theives.

The trail drops about 50 feet to the beach and passes through a pandanus grove. Under the shade of the hala, or screwpine (Pandanus odoratissimus), is an idyllic spot to picnic. As previously noted, the hala is frequently called "tourist pineapple" since the fruit resembles a pineapple. The fruit is sometimes cut into sections, which are then strung to make a fruit lei. The leaves, called lauhala, are dried and woven into mats and hats which are popular for beach and casual wear.

Swimming should be approached with caution due to the strong offshore currents. If you follow the rock-laden shore around the east side of the beach, you have a panorama of Hanalei Bay and the Princeville development on the far eastern cliff.

Hala — "Tourist Pineapple"

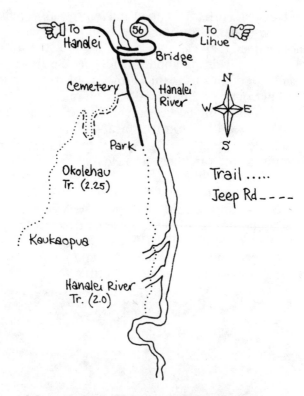

Hanalei River/Okolehau
(Hiking Area No. 3)

Rating: See individual hikes.

Features: Swimming, bamboo forest, fruit, views, historical sites.

Permission: None.

Hiking Distance & Time: See individual hikes.

Driving Instructions:
To Hanalei River Trail - 31 miles, 3/4 hour from Lihue. North on Route 56, then left on road after crossing the bridge in Hanalei Valley. Drive to road's end (1.9 miles) and park.

To Hanalei/Okolehau Trail - 30 miles, 3/4 hour from Lihue. North on Route 56, then left on road after crossing the bridge in Hanalei Valley. Drive 0.5 miles to paved road on right, turn right and drive 0.1 mile and park off the road in front of the cemetery.

Introductory Notes: The Hanalei (lit., "crescent bay") area is rich in history, having been a large Hawaiian community where taro was grown to support the population. Later, many Chinese settlers came to cultivate rice in the valley. During the missionary period, numerous experiments were conducted in efforts to cultivate coffee, silk, cotton and oranges. Oranges were once shipped to California where they had commercial value until oranges began to be grown there. During the 1850's, the harbor was an important port for whaling and trading ships. Rice, taro and cattle were exported. In this century during prohibition, liquor was distilled in the hills overlooking Hanalei.

The two hikes in Hanalei Valley are pleasurable, interesting and quite different. The hike into the valley is a pleasant, cool trek through an area rich in native and introduced plants with a generous variety of fruits to enjoy. It is possible to traverse the two miles only if the water level in the river is sufficiently low to allow crossing. DO NOT attempt to cross the river during times of high water or when rain is falling in the upper river valley. During the summer, 1988, the State Division of Forestry expected to complete the trail, to mark it, and to build a trail shelter/campsite.

The Hanalei Okolehau Trail is much different. It ascends about 1,300 feet along a ridge line to several vista points from which picturesque views of Hanalei and the coastline are possible. It is a hot, strenuous hike but worth every foot of effort.

Hanalei River Trail, 2 miles, 1 hour, (hike rating: hardy family).

As you approach the trailhead, you are passing through taro fields that have been cultivated for many years. The route follows a jeep road used by hunters. In the early morning it is common to meet pig hunters with their dogs hunting the small pig which is a popular sport with locals. A number of large mango trees border the road. Also look for oranges, guavas and delicious pomelo (Citrus maxima) trees which yield a large cantaloupe-sized fruit that has the aroma and taste of both grapefruit and orange. Both locals and tourists seek out these tasty treats, so the pickings are sometimes lean. Additionally, you will find a variety of flowers, particularly the small, delicate, purple mountain orchid and the aromatic ginger. Yellow giner (Zingiber zerumbet) is prolific along the road, and is easy to identify by the delicately fragrant, light yellow blossom that rises at the end of a narrow tube just behind an olive-colored bract. The leaves are a luxuriant green.

Bear to the left off the end of the road, pass through a gate in the fence and follow the trail to the first of two streams that enter the river. A small but magnificent bamboo forest surrounds you, and a cacophony of sounds is heard when the wind rushes through the dense growth. Bamboo has long been an important product on the Islands, having been used for fuel, furniture, musical instruments, utensils, building material and paper. And bamboo sprouts are commonly eaten on the Islands as a vegetable.

Shortly, you cross another stream and go through another bamboo forest with the river a short distance beyond. At the 1 1/2-mile point it is necessary to ford the river. If the water level is high in the river or if it is rainy in the back of the valley, it is best not to proceed for safety reasons. You'll find a number of large mango trees along the river bank from which locals have suspended ropes so that the daring can swing out over the river and drop into the cool water. The river crossing is at a big bend in the river where the trail ends on the east side at a trail shelter that was constructed in the summer of 1988.

A trail of sorts continues into the valley, but it is not marked or taped. It is used largely by pig hunters. The Division of Forestry has plans to take the trail another two miles up river.

Hanalei/Okolehau, 2.25 miles, 2 hours, 1272 feet gain, (hike rating: strenuous)

This trail gets its name from the valley and from the fact that during prohibition, Okolehau, a Hawaiian liquor distilled from the roots of the Hawaiian ki plant, was produced here. Many of the plants can still be found growing along the trail. Indeed, copper tubing was found in the area when the trail was being worked, according to the district forester.

The trail follows the powerline road to the left of the cemetery. The road is the most difficult part of the hike since portions of the route are approximately a 25% grade. The road, shaded by large silk oak, koa and mango trees, ends about 0.7-mile at a large powerline structure. Happily, strawberry guava can be found among the big trees and when in season this red, golf ball-sized fruit is a delightful treat. From roads end, you'll get your first view of Hanalei, the valley, the pali (cliffs) the river, and the bay. Wow! It's a sight to sooth the spirit.

From the powerline, the foot trail begins west of the road and ascends the ridge passing through a stand of Norfolk Island Pine, eucalyptus, ki and lots of strawberry guava. In 1988, the forestry service worked and taped the trail and expected to complete their work and a trail shelter at the summit in the summer.

Numerous vista points provide marvelous views of the Hanalei area. One of the best spots to pause is at the 1.7-mile point on a flat place where you'll find a geological survey marker. From here it's 0.5-mile to Kaukaopua (lit., "the horizon clouds alight") the summit marked by a "FR/TR" post. It's here that the Division of Forestry plans a trail shelter. The panorama is a rich reward after a hot hike.

Hanalei Bay from Okolehau Trail

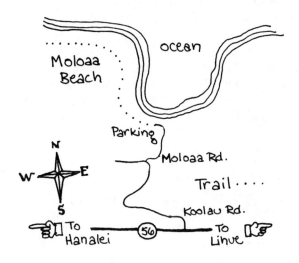

Moloaa Beach
(Hiking Area No. 4)

Rating: Family.

Features: Swimming, shells, fishing, fruits, views.

Permission: None.

Hiking Distance & Time: 1.5 miles, 1 hour.

Driving Instructions: 18 miles, 1/2 hour from Lihue. North on Route 56 for 16.6 miles, right on Koolau Road for 1.2 miles, and right on Moloaa Road to end. Park along beach right-of-way.

Introductory Notes: The Moloaa (lit., "matted roots" - said to be of the paper mulberry growing here) Beach hike is included here because it is one of the more secluded beaches on the island — a place where you can explore, fish, hunt of shells, or swim without intrusion. Check the mango trees along Moloaa Road for ripe fruit. Unfortunately, most of the fruit is out of reach unless you have a fruit picker — a bamboo pole with a cloth basket attached to a loop at one end. Many locals carry a pole that can be extended like a fishing rod and folded when not in use.

If you drive Moloaa Road at night, perhaps you shouldn't carry fresh pork. Even some present-day Hawaiians believe that the Demigod Kamapuaa, who is part pig, part man, still lives in the valley and will assume a variety of shapes and attack if he smells fresh pork. He can be outwitted, however, if the meat is wrapped in ti leaves.

On the Trail: You might hike the beach in search of shells or, with some luck, you might find a glass-ball float used by Japanese fishermen on their nets. Some break loose and make the long journey to Kauai.

The trail along the northwest side of the bay, a fisherman's trail, leads to some of the best spots from which to cast. Usually you need to walk out on the coral. Before you do, however, sit on the bank a while and watch the ocean to study the surf conditions. The only company you are likely to have is an occassional fisherman or the cattle or horses that graze on the slopes.

On the upper slopes you can idenify the paper mulberry (Broussonetia papyrifera) from which the name of the area is derived. It is a small tree with lobed leaves covered with woolly hairs on the undersides of the leaves. The bark of the plant was an important source of tapa, the cloth of ancient Hawaii. Tapa was made by removing the outer bark of the tree and soaking and beating the inner bark. A carved wooden mallet was used to pound the fibers until they became thin and flexible. Sheets were joined by the same pounding process, usually performed by men, while the women would decorate the cloth using a block printing method or leaves dipped in dye and pressed on the cloth.

The trail on the east side of the bay also snakes along the coast and provides a number of places to fish, picnic or simply enjoy the solitude.

Mangos — soooo good!

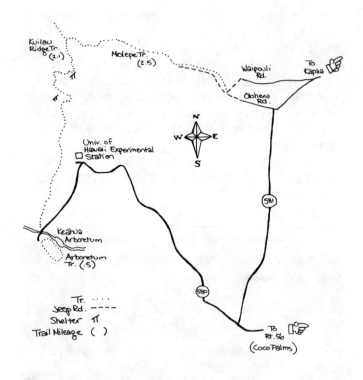

Keahua Trails
(Hiking Area No. 5)

Rating: See individual hikes.

Features: Swimming hole, native and introduced plants, fruits, picnic shelters.

Permission: None.

Hiking Distance & Time: See individual hikes.

Driving Instructions:

To Keahua Arboretum and Kuilau trails, 12 miles, 1/2 hour from Lihue. North on Route 56, left on Route 580 to University of Hawaii Agriculture Experiment Station, left on paved road (1.8 miles) to Keahua Stream. Kuilau Ridge Trailhead is on the right at a small turnout just before the stream and Keahua Arboretum Trailhead is on the left just past the stream opposite a parking area.

To Moalepe Trail, 12 miles, 1/2 hour from Lihue. North from Lihue on Route 56, left on Route 580, right on Route 581 (1.6miles) to pavement end and intersection with Waipouli Road. Park on shoulder of road.

Introductory Notes: The three hiking trails in the Keahua area offer some pleasurable experiences. They offer some marvelous views of the eastside coastline and of the Makaleha Mountains. Since the Moalepe Trail intersects the Kuilau Ridge Trail, you have an opportunity to follow the latter trail to Keahua Arboretum where you can hike and enjoy a delightful swimming hole.

Keahua Arboretum, .5 miles, 1/2 hour, (hike rating: family).

Keahua (lit., "the mound") Arboretum is a project of the Hawaii State Department of Land and Natural Resources, Division of Forestry. Here is a good chance to view a variety of native and introduced plants and to swim in a cool, fresh-water pool. The arboretum receives an annual average rainfall of 95 inches. The State Forest Reserve area extends west to the top of Mt. Waialeale ("overflowing water"), the highest spot on Kauai and the wettest place on earth, with an average annual rainfall of 468 inches. It once received a record 628 inches!

Arboretum Trailhead

The trail begins opposite the parking lot under a
canopy of painted gum (Eucalyptus deglupta) trees
with a colorful bark. This tree species is native to the
Philippines and New Guinea. Behind the painted gum
trees are rose gum (Eucalyptus grandis), a tree from
Australia and less colorful than the painted gum.
Several other trees are easy to identify here. Two of
them are kukui (Aleurites moluccana) and milo
(Thespesia populnea). Kukui trees, also called candlenut trees, had several uses. The most noteworthy use
was the burning of its oily nuts for a light source.
Kukui is Hawaii's State Tree and identifiable by its
pale green leaf and its walnut-sized nuts. Today, as in
old Hawaii, the wood of the milo tree is prized for its
use in making beautiful umekes, or calabashes.

The trail passes several picnic shelters and parallels the stream and several good swimming holes. The Makaleha mountains to the west are the source watershed for the domestic water supply. Rain falling on the mountains percolates into the soil and is collected in tunnels for distribution into the county water system. Good forest cover increases infiltration of water into the soil. This not only helps to increase the ground water supply but it also helps prevent soil erosion and floods caused by surface run-off.

One of the most conspicuous trees along the trail is the hau (Hibiscus tiliaceus) whose dense tangle of limbs prohibits entry. This yellow-flowered hibiscus was an early Hawaiian introduced plant. Here, you will also find the most common native tree species in Hawaii, the ohia lehua (Metrosideros collina). Early Hawaiian uses for the wood of the ohia included house timbers, poi boards, idols and kapa beaters. In the early 1900's, railroad ties hewn from ohia logs were exported for use on the mainland. A favorite of Madame Pele (the goddess of volcanoes) the ohia is easily identifiable by its tufted red stamens that remind the visitor of the bottlebrush tree.

Streams in this forest reserve provide a home for native and introducd fish. The native Hawaiian Oopu lives here as well as smallmouth bass. Fresh-water Tahitian prawns, esteemed as a delicious food, can also be found here.

As you climb the hill, notice the native hala tree commonly called "tourist pineapple." Its stiltlke trunk and its fruit that resembles a pineapple make this tree easy to identify. The trail descends the hill where you can return to your car or, better yet, return to the stream for a swim. There is usually a rope suspended from a mango tree on the bank about 100 yards from the shelter. It's a fun place.

Moalepe Trail, 2.5 miles, 1.5 hours (hike rating: hardy family). Elevation gain 500 feet.

On the trail: Do not attempt to drive beyond the Olohena-Waipouli Road intersection because the road is deeply rutted and, when wet, very slippery. The first part of the trail is on a right-of-way dirt road over pasture land. The usually cloud-enshrouded Makaleha (lit., "eyes looking about as in wonder and admiration") Mountains rise majestically to the northwest. In fact, the State of Hawaii, Division of Forestry, which is in charge of the area, has plans to extend the trail to the top of the Makalehas. Be sure to pause to enjoy the panorama of the coastline, from Moloaa on the north to Lihue on the south. There are some guavas along the fence and even more in the pasture, which is

Shelter on Kuilau Ridge Trail

private land. The trail is a popular equestrian route with riders who rent horses from the ranches in the area: evidence of this fact can be found on the trail!

The first mile is a gentle ascent in open country. Then the trail enters the forest reserve. Hereafter, the trail is bordered with a variety of plants and trees, including the wild, or Plilippine, orchid, different types of ferns, eucalyptus trees and the popular ohia lehua, with its pretty red blossoms. In the forest reserve the road-trail narrows and begins to twist and turn along the ridge, with many small and heavily foliated gulches to the left and Moalepe (lit., "chick with comb") Valley to the right. You can expect rain and therefore a muddy trail to the end of the hike. The trail reaches a junction with the Kuilau Ridge trail on a flat, open area at the 2- mile point. The ridge trail to the south (left) descends to two trail shelters and eventually ends at Keahua Arboretum, 2.1 miles from the junction. There is a sheltered picnic site 0.2 mile south of the junction along the Kuilau Ridge Trail. From the junction the Moalepe Trail is a footpath that snakes northwestward for 0.4 mile along Kuilau Ridge to a lookout point from which an enchanting panorama awaits the hiker.

Kuilau Ridge Trail, 2.1 miles, 1 1/2 hours (trail rating: hardy family).

One of the most scenic hiking trails on the island, the Kuilau ("to string together leaves or grass") Ridge Trail climbs the ridge from Keahua Arboretum to two vista-point picnic sites. From the trailhead to trail's end, an abundance of native and introduced plants greets the hiker. The ascent of the ridge is on a well-maintained foot and horse trail lined with hala, ti plants, from which hula skirts are fashioned, and the very pretty lavender wild, or Philippine orchid. But the best prize is a couple of mountain apple trees on the left side of the trail a short distance up from the trailhead. Perhaps you'll find some apples, which are red or pink when ripe.

At the 1 1/4-mile point the trail reaches a large flat area and a trail shelter and a picnic site. It is a delightful place to pause to enjoy views of the many gulches and the Makaleha Mountains beyond. However, if you plan to picnic, continue on for 0.8 mile to the second trail shelter and picnic area. The trail to the second shelter passes through one of the most beautiful places on the whole island. The Kuilau Ridge Trail twists and turns on a razorback ridge past a number of small waterfalls. It is a treasure to savor. Before reaching the shelter, the trail crosses a footbridge at the bottom of a gulch and then ascends the ridge to a large flat area and the picnic spot. From here, the trail continues 0.2 mile to its junction with the Moalepe Trail.

Arboretum rope swing — your turn

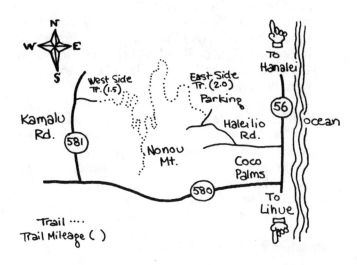

Trail ····
Trail Mileage ( )

Nonou Mountain (Sleeping Giant)
(Hiking Area No. 6)

Rating: Hardy Family.

Features: Views of Kauai, fruits.

Permission: None.

Hiking Distance & Time: Consult individual hikes.

Driving Instructions:
To east side trailhead — 7 miles, 1/4 hour from Lihue.

North from Lihue on Route 56 past Coco Palms
Hotel, left on Haleilio Road for 1.2 miles, park off
road by sign "Nonou Trail."

To west side trailhead — 10 miles, 1/2 hour from
Lihue. North from Lihue on Route 56, left on
Route 580, right on Route 581 (Kamalu Road) for
1.2 miles to sign "Nonou Trail" opposite 1055
Kamalu Road.

Introductory Notes: There are two routes to the
summit of Nonou (lit., "throwing") mountain both of
which are good, well-maintained trails that will take
you to the giant's chin and to his forehead. Nonou is
truly one of the best hikes on Kauai. Be sure to carry
one quart of water, since it is a hot hike in spite of
frequent trade winds.

Puni — The "Friendly Giant"

Bread fruit

It is told that the giant Puni lived among the legendary small folk, the Menehune, but was so clumsy that he continually knocked down their homes and their stone walls. Nevertheless, he was so friendly that the Menehune could not help but like him. One day the little people were faced with an invasion, and they went to the giant in the hope that he would destroy their enemies. However, they found him asleep on a ridge near Kapaa (lit., "the solid or the closing"). In an effort to awaken him, they threw large rocks on his stomach, which rebounded toward the ocean, destroying some of the invading canoes and causing the others to flee. In the morning they tried to awaken Puni again, only to discover that some of the rocks they had thrown at him had landed in his mouth. Tragically, he had swallowed them and died in his sleep.

East-side Trail, 2 miles, 1 1/2 hours, 1,250 feet gain.
Walk up the driveway about 20 yards to the trailhead sign on the left side. The trail is a series of well-
defined switchbacks along the northeast side of the
mountain. Pause frequently and enjoy the vistas overlooking the east side of Kauai. Below you lie the
Wailua Houselots, while the Wailua River and the
world famous Coco Palms resort are to your front
right. There are 1/4-mile trail markers along the entire
route.

The large trees that flourish in the area not only
offer a relatively shady trail, but also provide some
shelter from showers. You will find strawberry guava,
passion fruit, ti, tree ferns, a variety of eucalyptus, and
other flora that deserve special note.

The hau (Hibiscus tiliaceus) tree is of particular
interest not only because of its pretty bright-yellow
blossom but also because of its long, sinuous branches
that interlock to form an impenetrable barrier. Locals
jokingly note that the tree is appropriately named (hau,
pronounced how) because where they are plentiful, no
one knows "hau" to pass through!

On a spacious overlook at about the one-mile
point, you can rest in the shade of the ironwood
(Casuarina equisetifolia) tree, which resembles a pine
because of its long, slender, drooping, dull-green
needles. It is an introduced tree that has a long life and
is very useful as a windbreak or shade tree.

Just beyond the 1 1/2-mile marker, the west-side
trail merges with ours for the ascent to the summit. Alii
(lit., "chief") Shelter and table at the 1 3/4-mile marker
is a pleasant place to picnic and to enjoy the panorama
of the island and the solitude. There are a number of
benches near the shelter that provide comfortable
places to meditate. You should see a white-tailed
tropic bird (Phaethon lepturus) as it soars along the

mountain-side with its conspicuous 16-inch tail stream-ers.

From the shelter, walk south through the mon-keypod trees to survey the trail to the giant's "chin," "nose" and "forehead" that leads a short 1/2-mile to the summit. Be cautious as you walk across the narrow ridge above a nearly vertical 500-foot cliff, scramble up about 50 feet on your hands and knees to the "chin" and walk on a narrow ridge about 150 yards to the "forehead." From all points of the giant's anatomy, the views are outstanding. Look below the giant's chin for a hole through which the wind rushes.

West-side Trail, 1.5 miles, 1 hour, 1,000 feet gain.

The west-side trail is a bit shorter and not as steep, and offers more shade than the east-side trail. This trail passes by Queen's Acres and across a cattle range before entering the forest reserve. You will hike through a variety of introduced trees much like those found on the east side.

Look for the wild, or Philippine, orchid (Spathog-lottis plicata). The wild variety is usually lavender, with what appear to be five starlike petals, but are actually two petals and three sepals.

The trails join at the 1 1/2-mile marker for the short trek to Alii Shelter and on to the summit (see East-side Trail description for details).

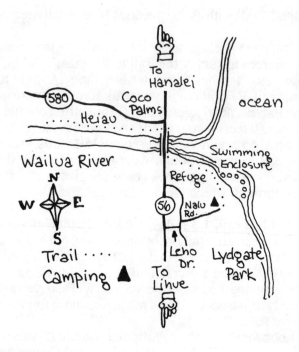

Lydgate Park
(Hiking Area No. 7)

Rating: Family

Features: Swimming, a heiau, a place of refuge, picnicking, fruits.

Permission: None.

Hiking Distance & Time: 1 mile, 1 hour.

Driving Instructions: 6 miles, 1/4 mile from Lihue. North from Lihue on Route 56, right on Leho Dr. at 5-mile marker, right on Nalu Road to parking by picnic area.

On the Trail: The Lydgate area has it all: hiking, wading, swimming, picnicking, and a bit of Hawaiiana. Begin your hike along the beach in front of the pavillion. If you begin at daybreak, you may be fortunate enough to find some glass ball floats, which are highly prized by locals, who will even search for them at night with lanterns. Most of these floats are from the nets of the Japanese fishermen, so they have traveled thousands of miles. Some have been found more that 30 inches in circumference.

Strawberry guava — yum, yum!

A short way north, the park's swimming enclosure is for children and the only safe place to swim. There are strong currents in this area, and an unusually heavy surf. Frequently, the rescue squad is called to help swimmers in distress who fail to heed the warning signs on the beach. The most famous of all rescues took place when Frank Sinatra was pulled from the surf by some local boys.

Between the swimming enclosure and the Wailua (lit., "two waters") River are the remains of a Temple of Refuge, a place of importance in old Hawaii. Each island had a place of refuge where those who had been vanquished in battle, violators of tabus, and noncombatants could find safety from capture or punishment. These havens were respected by all. After a period of time and prayer, the individual could return home — a very humane concept and practice.

Occasionally, when the ocean currents remove the sand, petroglyphs are visible on a group of black rocks below the temple. Their significance and meaning remain a mystery.

From here it is a short hike over the bridge then across the river to Route 580 on the northside. The road goes between the river and the Coco Palms Resort.

From the junction, follow the road 0.2 mile to Holo-Holo-Ku (lit., "to run-and-stand") Heiau (a place of worship) on the left side of the road. Heiaus played an important part in pre-Christian Hawaiian culture. There are hundreds of known heiaus on the Islands that served specifically to ensure rain, good crops, or success in war, while others were used for human sacrifice. Here you'll find a large sacrificial stone forming the southwest corner of the heiau. As you stroll through the heiau bear in mind that it is a religious place and should be respected as such.

Other points of interest in the heiau are the royal birthstones, a priest's house, and reproductions of idols. The originals are to be found in the Bishop Museum in Honolulu. Royal birthstones were important in ancient Hawaii. Pregnant women in the royal family would visit a heiau to unsure the royal status of an unborn infant.

A large mango tree across the road should be checked for fresh fruit, although the mangoes may be inaccessible unless you have a picker.

Follow the sign to a small public cemetery behind the heiau which contains a number of lava headstones. Beyond the cemetery through the brush are a number of vistas which provide views of the Wailua River.

Temple of Refuge

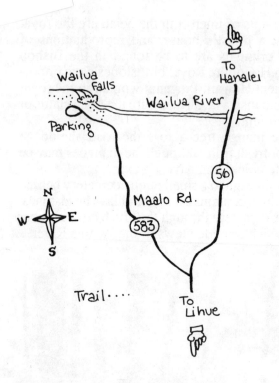

Wailua Falls
(Hiking Area No. 8)

Rating: Strenuous.

Features: Swimming, fruit, waterfall.

Permission: None.

Hiking Distance & Time: .5 mile, 1/2 hour.

Driving Instructions: 5 miles, 1/2 hour from Lihue. North on Route 56, left on Route 583 (signed Wailua Falls) to 0.2 mile before reaching the end of the road.

Introductory Notes: The power and beauty of Wailua (lit., "many waters") Falls after a heavy rain are awesome. Locals probably visit the falls as much as do tourists. Periodically, some daring-foolish individual reenacts the ancient practice of diving into the pool below from atop the falls. Hawaiian chiefs at one time would dive from the falls on a wager or to prove their courage. DO NOT JUMP FROM ATOP THE FALLS. Several persons have been killed in recent years. Wailua Falls is now recognized by people throughout the world since it was was as the opening scene for the popular television series,"Fantasy Island."

On the Trail: The trailhead begins 0.2 mile before the guard rail at the end of the road. A large dirt turnout where you can park marks the point of the trailhead. The hike to the pool below the falls is short but not without some difficulty and hazard. An extremely steep trail descends from the road to the stream. When wet, which it usually is, the steep trail is very slippery and dangerous. The trail makes an abrupt drop to the stream so BE CAUTIOUS. Once at the stream, walk left along the bank to the pool below the falls.

Before you swim under the falls, consider the fact that rocks and debris are carried in the water over the falls. It's a delightful place to picnic and to swim and to watch the ever-present white-tailed tropic birds soaring about just below the falls.

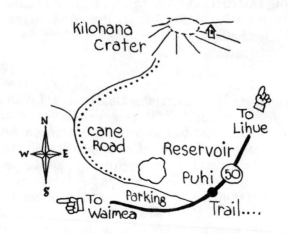

Kilohana Crater
(Hiking Area No. 9)

Rating: Hardy family.

Features: Panoramic views, fruits.

Permission: Lihue Plantation Co., Ltd., 245-7325.

Hiking Distance & Time: 2.5 miles, 1 1/2 hours, 1000 foot elevation gain.

Driving Instructions: 4 miles, 1/4 hour from Lihue. South from Lihue on Route 50 to a turnout on a sugar cane road. Look for a large reservoir just off the main cane road and park on the shoulder. If the sugar cane is mature, you cannot see the reservoir from the road, but there is no mistaking the wide turnout/parking place just past the 4-mile marker.

Introductory Notes: Kilohana (lit., "lookout point") was once the site of a weekend retreat for company employees. The remains of a house are on the northeast side of the summit. Legend records that Lahi, a young boy, while hunting birds with his uncle, slew a giant. When warriors came to avenge the death of the giant, the boy hid and threw one at a time over the cliff into the caldera.

On the Trail: The entire trail follows the main cane road, from which you will probably see a variety of cane operations. The sugar-cane cycle includes planting, growth, irrigation, pest control, tasseling (removing blossoms), burning off (tourching the field to burn away dead growth, weeds and leaves), and harvesting over a period of 18-21 months. You will not see the

Kilohana Crater

irrigation systems that are common on other islands, since most of the cane in the upland regions depends on rainfall for water.

As you hike, the summit is to the front-right. Hike west on the cane road that swings right as you approach your destination. There is no shade before the summit, so it is a good idea to wear a hat and to use sun screen/lotion.

The crater is ringed by strawberry guava (Psidium cattleianum). Between August and October this red, walnut-sized fruit flourishes. It may be eaten whole, or after removing the small seeds found inside. The crater is relatively shallow and overgrown with a variety of vegetation; the reward of the trip is the sweeping views of the island, particularly the middle valley region of the east side.

Follow the road to the abandoned house on the northeast side to see some outstanding examples of monkeypod trees (Sameanea saman). The wood of this tree should be familiar to visitors for it is widely purchased for gifts in the form of carved bowls and trays so typical of Hawaii. A symmetrical tree with tiny, delicate pink tufts, the monkeypod will blossom in May and June. The leaves consist of tiny, fernlike leaflets not unlike those of the shower tree. With ample water, it is not uncommon for a monkeypod tree to grow to 80 feet.

In 1882, the Lihue Plantation began a large-scale reforestation program and hired a German forester named Lange to do the job at Kilohana. Consequently, the crater is sometime referred to as the "German Forest." Ironwood (Casuarina equisetifolia) was planted to replace dying kukui trees. Although ironwood has little commercial value, it is an excellent windbreak. It resembles a pine because of its long, slender, drooping, dull-green needles.

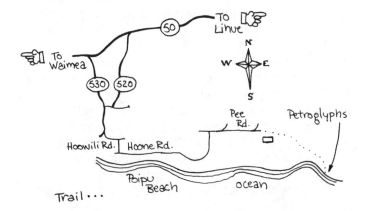

Poipu Beach Petrogylphs
(Hiking Area No. 10)

Rating: Family.

Features: Petroglyphs, burial grounds, swimming, views.

Permission: None.

Hiking Distance & Time: 1 mile, 1/2 hour.

Driving Instructions: 14 miles, 1/2 hour from Lihue.
South on Route 50, left on Route 520, right on
Route 530, quick left on Poipu Beach Road, right
on Hoowili Road, left on Hoone Road, and left on
Pee Road to end of the pavement. Drive 50 yards
on dirt road to end. Park.

Introductory Notes: The sea and sand covers the
petroglyphs so that they can only be seen during
periods of low tide. Poipu (lit., "completely overcast
of crashing — as waves") Beach is perhaps the finest
swimming, snorkeling, surfing and body-surfing area
on Kauai. In addition to taking the hike below, you
should plan to swim and picnic along Poipu Beach
Road. Be certain to try body-surfing or Bogie-board-
ing at Brennecke's Beach, where the big waves give
you an exhilarating ride.

On the Trail: From the trailhead, you can see a
crescent-shaped bay. Your destination is the bluff at
the far end of the beach. The hike begins on the most
recent volcanic eruption on Kauai, about 40,000 years
ago! Young in geologic time anyway, the area is
dotted with numerous cinder cones and lava tubes,
which some say extend to the ocean. Indeed as you
walk on the hard lava surface, you can sometime hear
and feel the rushing water underfoot.

Hike the sandy road to the beach and walk along
the shoreline. All the plants here struggle for survival
in an area where the rainfall is light and the soil
extremely porous. Ilima (Sida fallax) is a small, woody
shrub that grows wild. With its small, blunt, bright
green leaves and its pale orange, orange or brown
flowers, it makes a popular lei. In earlier times only

members of the royalty were allowed to wear an ilima lei.

Follow the coast line above Makahuena (lit., "eyes overflowing heat") sand dunes, where in ancient times common people were buried. Children particularly enjoy rolling or sliding down the dunes and hiding in the sanstone caves in ledges along the coast. Find the sandstone ledge at the far end of the beach. Unless the sea or the sand covers them, you will find petroglyphs in the form of human figures, boats, and abstract images that remain a mystery to the experts.

Snorkeling at Poipu

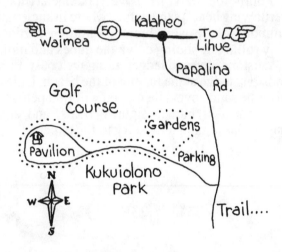

Kukuiolono Park
(Hiking Area No. 11)

Rating: Family.

Features: Japanese Garden, picnic, views.

Permission: None.

Hiking Distance & Time: 1/2 mile, 1/2 hour.

Driving Instructions: 12 miles, 1/2 hour from Lihue.
South from Lihue on Route 50 to Kalaheo, left on
Papalina Road (1 mile), right at park gate and park
by gardens.

Introductory Notes: Walter McBryde, son of one of the earliest European settlers on Kauai, built his home and an elegant park on this hill above the town of Kalaheo (lit., "the proud day") and overlooking Lawai (lit., "seaward") and the beautiful south coast. Today the McBryde estate is a private park and a popular spot to golf, picnic, and stroll through a Japanese garden. Kukuiolono (lit., "the light of the god Lono") is so named because the hill was used by ancient Hawaiians to signal fishermen at sea and to serve as a beacon.

On the Trail: Park by the garden and take the short, interesting, pleasant loop around the gardens. The legendary stones of the Hawaiians are particularly notable. The name of each stone indicates its use or significance. For example, there are Lono's Spoon Stone, Awa (fish) Stone, Kauai Iki (little Kauai) Stone (shaped like Kauai), Stone Bowl and Stone Salt Pan. Most are three to four feet in circumference. There are also a number of smaller "game stones" which were used in Hawaiian games similar to bowling and the shotput.

The flora in the garden is a mixture of native and introduced plants and trees: crotons, mangoes, kukuis, bananas, papayas, tree ferns, sego pines, and other types of pines, to name a few. The most striking sights are the intricate and delicately beautiful bonsai plants and the flowing "dry stream" of white stone that passes through the garden.

During World War ll, the "Big House" of the McBrydes was on the hill overlooking the garden. The house was used to billet U.S. military officers who were on leave. The house burned down many years ago.

From the garden, walk up the road to the pavilion. You will enjoy the plumeria (Plumeria acutifolia) trees along the road. Every color and shade of plumeria seems to be represented. Perhaps the most popular of all lei flowers, the thick, velvety flowers are long-lasting and have a fine fragrance. The white, yellow, pink and cerise plumerias are overwhelming when in full bloom. The milky juice, however, is poisonous and will stain clothing.

The road passes through the golf course, so be on the lookout for flying white balls. You will find water, picnic tables, shelter, and restrooms at the pavilion at the summit: a perfect place to picnic and enjoy the panorama.

Stone Bowl

Waimea (Russian Fort)
(Hiking Area No. 12)

Rating: Family.

Features: Historic site, driftwood, swimming, views.

Permission: None.

Hiking Distance & Time: 1/2 mile, 1/2 hour.

Driving Instructions: 22 miles, 3/4 hour from Lihue. South on Route 50 to sign "Fort Elisabeth" just before the Waimea River.

On the walls — Russian fort

Introductory Notes: In 1817 the Russians secured a foothold on the islands with the construction of a fort that overlooked the Waimea (lit., "reddish water") River and the sea. Like the Hawaiians, the Russians ·used a dry-construction method in which rocks are fitted according to shape, without mortar. The fort was christened Fort Elisabeth[*sic*]. The State of Hawaii has constructed an interpetive exhibit at the trailhead and provides a trail guide to the fort. Across the river on the west side is the town of Waimea and the site of Captain Cook's first landing in Hawaii.

On the Trail: A path leads from the display along the north side of the fort to the river and then into the fort. The thick walls of the fort enable the visitor to walk on top of them for the best view of the fort. A strong imagination is necessary to mentally reconstruct the fort, for the walls and the interior are in disrepair after many years of neglect. A trail snakes through the remains of the fort to the south side, and to the mouth of the river and the beach. One can easily see the commanding position of the fort.

Both inside and outside the fort are a variety and abundance of dried flowers and an assortment of dried "weeds" that make a pretty floral arrangement. Hike from the mouth of the river along the gray-black sand beach to see some interesting driftwood.

Offshore to the southwest lies the tiny island of Niihau, part of Kauai County, which is privately owned by the Robinson family, whose ancestor bought the island for $10,000 in 1864 from the Hawaiian monarchy. Some point to Niihau as the last place where pure Hawaiians live as their ancestors did. Others, applying today's standards, assert that the people live primatively and under outrageous conditions. The controversy is heightened by the fact the outside world is mostly excluded; visits are by invitation only.

Be certain to return to the bridge for impressive views up the river into Waimea Canyon.

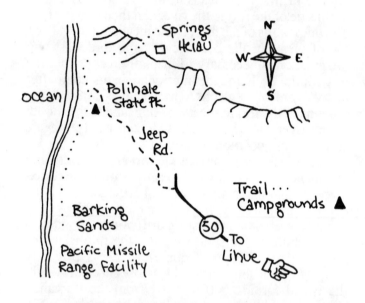

Polihale State Park
(Hiking Area No. 13)

Rating: Hardy family.

Features: Camping, swimming, heiau.

Permission: Camping permits from State Parks (see Appendix).

Hiking Distance & Time: 3 miles, 1 1/2 hours.

Driving Instructions: 38 miles, 1 hour from Lihue. South on Route 50 to sign "Polihale State Park" just before the end of the highway. Left at the sign and follow the dirt/sugar-cane road for 4.7 miles to the park.

Introductory Notes: Polihale (lit., "house bosom") State Park is a relatively secluded place to camp. As at all state parks, camping is free and is limited to five days per month. In recent years, some campers have been violated by local men here so that you should be cautious. DO NOT camp alone and secure your valuables.

This was once the site of a famous heiau — a pre-Christian place of worship. The remains, in the form of distinctive rock piles, can be seen along the slopes of the cliffs above the park. Here you can enjoy the sunset and the view of the island of Niihau and Lehua to its

Beach camping

right. The latter is in fact a big rock. In legend Lehua is considered to have been the first landing place of Pele, the fire goddess. The name comes from the story that Pele's sister, Hiiaka, placed a lei of lehua blossoms on it.

On the Trail: From the camping area, it is a hot 3-mile hike south to barking sands beach. Unless you are a sun worshipper, sun protection is well-advised since there is no relief from the hot sun. Wear shorts or hike in a bathing suit for you will want to splash in the surf and take frequent dips in the ocean. Swimming, however, should be approached with caution for the sea can be treacherous, with riptides most of the year.

The beach on the way to the sand dunes is somewhat isolated and, therefore, uncrowded. In fact, you probably will not see another person until you reach barking sands. Military personnel and their guests visit the dunes from the U.S. Navy missile facility just south of barking sands.

The barking sand dunes are easy to identify, for some are as high as 60 feet and about 1/2 mile in area. The name "barking sands" comes from the idea that the sand can be made to give off a dog-like "bark" or "woof" sound. Some visitors have not "heard" a sound and therefore doubt the whole notion, while others insist that they have "heard" a sound, whatever it is. Whatever the fact, try your luck. One of the following methods may be successful for you. 1) Find a dry dune and slide down on foot. While sliding, listen for a deep, sonorous "woofing" sound. 2) Fill a bottle about two-thirds full with sand, shake it, and listen for a sound. 3) Stomp up and down on the side of any dune. After trying all these methods, you are either pleased and fascinated by the "sounds" that you heard or you feel like a damn fool!

Kokee State Park/Waimea Canyon
(Hiking Area No. 14)

Rating: See individual hikes.

Features: Views of Waimea Canyon, Na Pali Coast and Kalalau Valley, swimming, camping, waterfalls, iliau plant, rain forest, wilderness hiking, and fruit.

Permission: Camping permits from State Parks and cabin reservations from Kokee Lodge (see Appendix).

Hiking Distance & Time: See individual hikes.

Driving Instructions: 38 miles, 1 1/2 hours from Lihue to Kokee State Park Headquarters. South on Route 50, right on Route 550 (Waimea Canyon Drive) past Waimea.

Introductory Notes: Kokee (lit., "to bend or to wind") State Park and Waimea (lit., "reddish water") Canyon are the most popular hiking and camping areas on the island, for obvious reasons. Waimea Canyon has been called the "Grand Canyon of the Pacific." Kokee has numerous hiking trails and untold hunting trails that snake along the pali (cliff) to otherwise remote and inaccessible places. Everyone is quite taken by the beauty and grandeur of Waimea Canyon. It is about one mile wide, 3600 feet deep, and 10 miles long. While it does not match the magnificence of the Grand Canyon in Arizona, it has its own unique magic, with its verdant valleys, its lush tropical forest and its rare birds and flora.

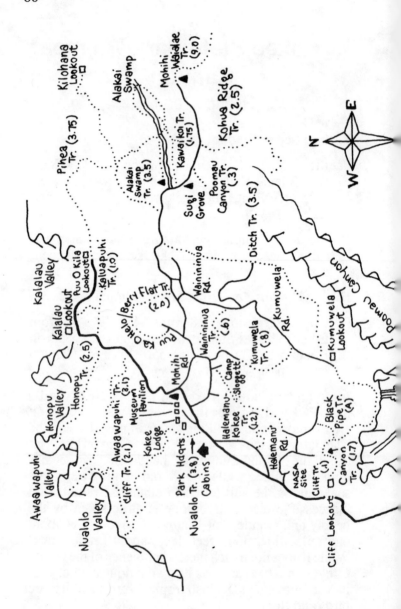

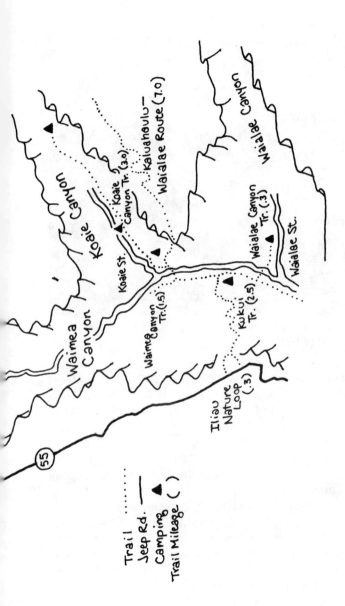

Trail ....
Jeep Rd. ____
Camping ▲
Trail Mileage ( )

Waimea Canyon

Technically, this northwest corner of the island is under two state agencies, the Division of State Parks and the Division of Forestry, both of which are under the Hawaii State Department of Land and Natural Resources; and Kokee Lodge is operated by a private concessionaire. While the accommodations are not luxurious, they are very comfortable and in keeping with the surroundings.

The state cabins at Kokee, very popular with locals and tourists, require reservations. Kokee Lodge is not really a lodge but rather 12 rustic cabins completely furnished with refrigerator, water heater, range, cooking utensils, shower, linens, blankets, beds and fireplace. All you need is food, which is not available at Kokee but 20 miles away in Waimea. There is, however, a restaurant and cocktail lounge a short walk from the cabins, open 8:30 a.m. to 5:30 p.m. and on Friday and Saturday evenings for dinner 6-9 p.m.

Each cabin will accommodate 3-7 persons at a very modest cost from $35-45 per day. The cabins are very popular with locals, so make reservations early — even one year in advance is not too soon. Write to the lodge for complete information and reservations (see Appendix).

At the north end of a shady, picturesque meadow, tent and trailer camping are available in the shade of tall eucalyptus trees. Caming, limited to five days, is free. Water, tables, barbecues, restrooms and cold-water showers are available. There are a number of wilderness camping areas and shelters available (see

Kokee cabins

the map and the trail descriptions) under the jurisdiction of the Division of Forestry.

In recent years a controversy has existed over the future of the Kokee-Waimea area. Conservationists have sought Federal legislation to establish a national park so that the wilderness can be preserved in relatively pristine condition. Opponents of this proposal seek to retain the present status, because a national park would probably prohibit hunting, land leases for vacation cabins and taking plants.

Whatever the future, whether your interest is hiking, hunting or sightseeing, no trip to Kauai is complete without a visit to Kokee and Waimea Canyon. Kokee is also the home of the rare mokihana berry (see the Pihea Trail below), and the even rarer and beautiful

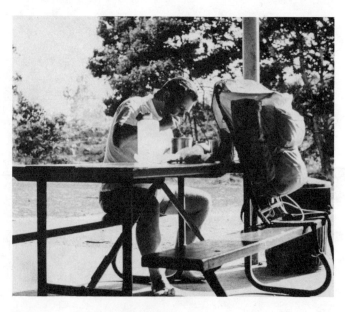

Camping — Kokee State Park

iliau tree (see the Iliau Nature Loop Trail below) and the delicious Methley plum, which is ready for picking throughout the park in late May or early June. The picking season is short because local people flock to the park and carry off buckets full of this delectable fruit. Since 1986, pickings have been poor because so many trees have been damaged by harvesters while others have been overwhelmed by other vegatation.

On the Trail: Although it is not required, for safety reasons you should sign in and out in the registry at the Kokee State park Headquarters when hiking. Your interests, physical condition, and length of stay at Kokee will help determine which hike you take. On the whole, trails in the general vicinity of park headquarters are relatively short and easy, while trails into Waimea Canyon, to the valley overlooks or into the Alakai Swamp are full-day or overnight trips. Access to most of the trails is from jeep roads that radiate off the main highway — Route 55. You should not travel these roads in a passenger car even when dry, because many are steep and deeply rutted. The ranger at park headquarters and the museum personnel are the best sources of information about road and trail conditions.

In 1987-8, the trails in the Kokee State Park/ Waimea Canyon area had been worked, brushed, posted, and taped so that they were in top condition. Much of the credit goes to Mac Hori, Kokee Park Supervisor, and to Ralph Daehler, District Forester. Their trail improvement programs have involved hundreds of student workers, unpaid volunteers, the Hawaii Sierra Club, and the State National Guard, 227th Engineer Company.

The mileage from Park Headquarters to the trailhead via the most direct road is noted preceding each trail description.

KOKEE — Southwest

Puu Ka Ohelo/Berry Flat Trail
Park HQ to trailhead 0.9mile.

An easy, pleasant loop trail off Mohihi (a variety of sweet potato) Road combines the Berry Flat and the Puu Ka Ohelo (Ohelo hill) trails. In 1988, the trailhead was posted and the trail was clear, broad and easy to follow. You will cross a couple of small streams along this verdant trail. The banana passion fruit (Passiflora mollissima) is found here draping from the trees. It is a a wild vine that produces a pretty, light-pink blossom and a small, yellow, banana-shaped fruit. The Park Service regards the vine as a pest because it smothers native trees.

Both trails pass through scenic forest containing mostly introduced trees that should be easy to identify. Particularly noteworthy is a stand of California redwoods (Seguoia simpervirens) that will excite the senses. These wondrous giants tower over the other trees adding a certain majesty to the grove and their droppings provide a luxuriant carpet on which to walk. They are found as you begin the Berry Flat Trail.

In addition, there are stands of Australian eucalyptus, Japanese Sugi pines and the native koa (Acacia koa), which grows to a height of more that 50 feet. The koa has a light gray bark that is smooth on young trees and considerably furrowed on mature trees. The leaves are smooth, stiff, and crescent-shaped. Often called Hawaiian mohogany, the wood is red with a wavy grain that makes it popular for use in furniture, woodwork and ukuleles. In older times it had nobler purposes, having been used for war canoes, surfboards and calabashes.

The prize to be sought here is the popular Methley plum that flourishes in the Kokee area. However, plum picking has been poor in recent years because of storm damage to the trees. Look for plum trees whose fruit ripens at the end of May or the first part of June.

There is also a variety of birds along both trails. (All bookstores on the island have small, pocket-sized, inexpensive bird books featuring the most frequently seen birds.) The cardinal (Richmondena cardinalis) is a commonly seen bird on the island which was introduced from the mainland. The male, with his

Rare Iliau blossom

all-red body and pointed crest, has been seen along the trail as well as throughout the park.

Black Pipe Trail, .4 mile, 1/2 hour (hiking rating: hardy family).
Park HQ to trailhead 2.5 miles.

This is a short spur trail that connects the Canyon Trail with the middle fork of the Halemanu Road. The trail descends into a small overgrown gulch and then climbs to follow the cliff to the Canyon Trail. It is along the pali that the rare and beautiful iliau (Wilkesia gymnoxiphium) grows. A relative to the rare silversword that grows on Maui, the iliau is endemic to Kauai and found only in the western mountains. It grows 4-12 feet high, it is unbranched, and the stems end in clumps of long, narrow leaves 6-16 inches long. Once in its life, the plant flowers in a flourish of hundreds of tiny yellow blossoms.

Canyon Trail, 1.7 miles, 2 hours (hike rating: strenuous).
Park HQ to trailhead 2.1 miles.

Although the Canyon Trail is steep in parts and requires some stamina, it offers some of the best views of Waimea Canyon. The trail begins at the Halemanu Road and runs south along the east rim of the canyon. It is somewhat precipitous in places, so be careful. At the Cliff Lookout, which is 0.1 mile beyond the end of the Halemanu Road, you get not only a view of the canyon, but also a view of the trail as it descends and snakes along the cliff.

The Canyon Trail is a popular hike. The trail descends into a gulch and snakes along the cliff to Kokee Stream and Waipoo (lit., "head water") Falls, where you can picnic in the shade and swim or splash in the stream. The best swimming hole is at the base of Waipoo Falls #1.

On the trail

A common plant on the high, dry ridges is the lantana (Lantana camara), which blossoms almost continuously. Its flowers vary in color from yellow to orange to pink or red; infrequently they are white with yellow centers. It is a low shrub with a thick, strong wood.

A small, pretty, yellow-green bird, the anianiau (Loxops parva), is common in the high forests of Kauai. In truth it is difficult for the less-than-expert to tell the difference between the anianiau and the amakihi (Loxops virents), which is the same size and yellow. However, if you get a close look, the amakihi has a dark loral (space between the eye and bill) mark that joins the eye and the curved dark bill. No matter, however, for they are both pretty birds.

From the falls, the trail makes a steep climb out of the gulch and ascends the pali, from which some of the best vistas of Waimea are had. Once again, be careful for while the trail is broad and easy to follow, at some places steep walls drop to the canyon below. There are numerous places to pause in some shade to enjoy the view through the canyon to the sea on the south side.

After a steep climb, the trail ends at Kumuwela Lookout, from where you can return on the Canyon Trail or connect with the Kumuwela Road or the Ditch Trail.

Cliff Trail, .1 mile, 10 minutes (hike rating: family).
Park HQ to trailhead 2.1 miles.

The Cliff Trail provides a scenic vista of Waimea Canyon and a convenient departure point for the Canyon Trail. It begins after a short walk or drive down the Halemanu Road. Be quiet as you approach the lookout so that you do not frighten any goats that might be browsing there. Ferel goats are commonly sighted here or walking along the pali area opposite the lookout.

Ditch Trail, 3.5 miles, 4 hours (hike rating: strenuous).
Park HQ to trailhead 2.3 miles.

Shortly after this trail was cleaned and posted in 1988, earth slides in two places damaged the path. Consequently, the Ditch Trail is, what it always has been, an ambitious hike over some very rough terrain. In any event, the trail follows a circuitous route along a cliff and in and out of numerous gulches and small stream canyons. It is best to enter this trail at the trailhead from Mohihi Road.

The trail offers spectacular sights of the interior of Waimaa, which is one of the broader and deeper of the canyons. Across the canyon you'll see Kohua Ridge, with its many falls and cascades during rainy periods. Awini ("sharp, bold, forward") Falls is at the southwest tip of the ridge, with Mohihi Falls to the right-rear of the canyon and Moeloa ("to oversleep") Falls to the left-rear of the canyon.

The trail is rich with flora, from the common guava to lehua and a variety of ferns. The variety of tree fern (Cibotium menziesii) seen here is the "monkey's tail" fern, with its wiry black hairs on the frond stems. It has the biggest trunk of all Hawaiian tree ferns, a trunk often used for carving akuas (idols) or tikis.

Halemau-Kokee Trail, 1.2 miles, 1 hour (hike rating: hardy family).
Park HQ to trailhead 0.6 mile.

This trail starts just before entering Camp Slogget near the old ranger station and ends on Halemanu Road. It's a hike for those who are interested in a short, pleasant, easy walk with the prospect of seeing some native birds and plants. The trail, linking Mohihi and Halemanu roads, is an enjoyable hike in itself and also a route to hiking areas on Kokee's west side.

Tall trees dominate the area, such as lehua and the majestic koa. There are three red birds that you can expect to see along the trail. The cardinal has a pronounced crest, which is the most prominent feature distinguishing it from the apapane (Himatione sanguinea), a deep-crimson bird with black wings and tail and a slighly curved black bill, and the iiwi (Vestiaria coccinea), a vermilion bird with black wings and tail and orange legs. The latter also has a rather pronounced curved salmon bill. Unless you get a good look at these birds, it is difficult to identify them, but they can be enjoyed without being identified. One other bird that is common throughout the forest is the elepaio (Chasiempis sanwichensis), an endemic bird that is grey-backed with a rather long, blackish tail and white rump. It is a somewhat noisy bird, giving forth with what is best described as a sort of "wolf-whistle."

Iliau blossoms — wow!

Iliau Nature Loop, .3 mile, 1/4 hour (hike rating: family).

Park HQ to trailhead 6.3 miles.

The nature loop is a good place to see some 20 endemic plants including the rare iliau (Wilkesia gymnoxiphium). A relative to the equally rare Maui silversword, the iliau is endemic to Kauai. It grows 4-12 feet high, it is unbranched, and the stems end in clumps of long, narrow leaves 6-16 inches long. Once in its life, the plant flowers in a flourish of hundreds of tiny yellow blossoms. At one time, the plants were identified by name plates, but they have all been destroyed or impossible to read because of weather damage. There is no missing the iliau, however, since hundreds flourish in a small area.

The trail provides a number of vistas for viewing the canyon and Waialae (lit., "mudhen water") Falls on the opposite, west wall of the canyon.

Kaluahaulu-Waialae Trail, 7 miles, full-day hike (hike rating: difficult).

Trailhead in Waimea Canyon.

This trail is CLOSED (1988), but it is scheduled to become part of an ambitious loop trail covering some 20 miles and extending from the visitor-center area, down Mohihi (Camp 10) Road, across the western portion of the Alakai Swamp, down into Waimea Canyon via Kaluahaulu hill and up the Kukui Trail to the main highway and back to the visitor center. Whew!

The Kaluahaulu-Waialae (lit., Kaluahaulu — "the reddish pit," and Waialae — "mudhen water") Trail is in disrepair and should not be attempted. The trail was originally constructed by the Civilian Conservation Corps in the 1930's, but erosion and hurricanes have

damaged much of the trail. Check with the Division of
Forestry regarding its current condition.
There is ample water in the canyon, but it should be
treated, filtered or boiled before drinking.

Kaluapuhi Trail, 1.0 miles, 1 hour (hike rating: family).
Park HQ to trailhead 1.9 miles.
   Access to the trail is a few feet off the main road
where a trail marker identifies the trailhead.
   Even though the Park Service claims that this trail
is "2.0+" miles, the last mile is overgrown with berry
bushes and is not passable (1988). The first mile of the
trail is wide and flat and easy to follow. At the 0.5-mile
point, an equally wide, flat trail goes left and emerges

Ginger blossoms

0.5 miles later, 0.2 miles northeast (right) of the Kalalau Lookout. This is a pleasant hike for the entire family with the prospect of sweet plums along the trail.

Kaluapuhi (lit., "the eel pit") Trail is a favorite during plum season. If it is a good year (poor 1986-88) for the delicious Methley plum, this trail will take you to some of the best trees. The pickings are generally good here due to the fact that the only access to the trees is on foot.

Plum picking is regulated by the state and is limited to 25 pounds of the fruit per person per day. Pickers must check in and out at the checking station, usually located near park headquarters. Many local people bring the whole family and stay overnight to get an early start.

Koaie Canyon Trail, 3 miles, 2 hours (hike rating: strenuous).

Trailhead is in Waimea Canyon.

Koaie Canyon is a favorite of hikers and back-packers, for it is an easier trail than Waimea Canyon Trail and it leads to a secluded wilderness shelter. The canyon's name comes from the koaie (Acacia koaia) tree, which is endemic to the islands and is much like the koa tree. The wood, however, is harder than koa wood, and was once used to make spears and fancy paddles.

If the water is high in Waimea Stream, you should not hike up-river, since it is necessary to cross the river to the east side to get on the Koaie Canyon Trail. You cross the river (posted in 1988) just below Poo Kaeha, a prominent hill about 500 feet above the river, pick up Koaie Stream a short distance later, and follow the south side of the stream into Koaie Canyon.

The canyon is a fertile area that was once exten-sively farmed, as is evidenced by the many terraced

Kukui Trailhead

areas you'll observe and the rock walls and the remains of house sites. You can ususlly find ample pools in the stream to swim in or at least to cool off in. During the summer months, the water is usually low, but sufficient for some relief from the hot canyon. The Division of Forestry has a number of wildland campsites here. At trail's end, you find Lonomea Camp, an open shelter with a table alongside the stream near a generous pool for swimming. The Lonomea (Sapindus cahuensis) is a native tree with ovate leaves which reaches heights of up to 30 feet. They grow only on Kauai and Oahu.

Don't forget to pack out your trash.

There is ample water in the canyon, but it should be treated, filtered or boiled before drinking.

Kukui Trail, 2.5 miles, 2 hours, 2000 feet gain (hike rating: strenuous).
Park HQ to trailhead 6.3 miles.

The Kukui (candlenut lamp) Trail is the only trail into Waimea Canyon. A Division of Forestry sign marks the trailhead both at the state highway and at the departure point off the Iliau Trail. Sign in and out on the trail register located near the trail's beginning. You may hike and camp in the canyon for three days.

The trail drops over 2000 feet into the canyon and in 1988, it was in good condition. The first half of the trail is open so that sun protection and a hat are advisable. If you hike during the heat of the day, I am certain you would rather be standing under Waialae Falls which can be seen tumbling from the pali across the canyon. About 0.3 mile down the trail, look for a wooded gulch on the left where several hibiscus (Hibiscus waimeae) trees are growing. This variety is an endemic tree that bears large white flowers that are so fragrant you can smell them from a distance.

You'll probably find numerous half-gallon plastic jugs along the trail. They are left by pig and goat hunters as they descend so they will have fresh water on their return. For safety reasons you should stay out of the brush so that you won't be mistaken for a goat or pig by hunters.

The first part of the hike offers some spectacular views of Waimea Canyon and the second part passes through heavy growth until it emerges at Wiliwili (a native tree bearing red seeds that make pretty necklaces) Camp along the boulder-laden banks of Waimea River. It is a delightful spot to camp in shade with ample water. Many hikers make a base camp at Wiliwili and then hike on the canyon trails and in the side canyons. If you are in good hiking condition, it is possible to make the hike in and out in one day.

There is ample water in the canyon, but it should be treated, filtered or boiled before drinking.

Kumuwela Trail, .8 mile, 1 hour, 300 feet gain (hike rating: hardy family).
Park HQ to trailhead 1.0 mile.

At the end of the short spur road off Mohihi Road (see map) turn left into the forest for the beginning of the Kumuwela Trail. The trailhead is marked (1988) and the trail is well-maintained. The trail dips abruptly into a luxuriant, fern-lined gulch where Kahili ginger (Hedychium coronarium) flourishes. The size, fragrance and light-yellow blossoms overwhelm most visitors. You should find many places on and off the trail where ferel pigs have been digging to get at roots.

Along this verdant trail there are also specimens of lantana, lilikoi (passion fruit) as well as handsome kukui and koa trees. The last .3 mile requires a 300-foot elevation to Kumuwela Road, where you can connect with the Canyon Trail.

Waialae Canyon Trail, .3 mile, 1/2 hour.
Trailhead in Waimea Canyon.

This short, undeveloped trail takes you south along Waimea River from the campground at the terminus of the Kukui Trail. A marker identifies the point where you can ford the river and enter lower Waialae Canyon. The trail follows the north side of Waialae Stream for a short distance to "Poachers Camp," where a shelter, table and pit toilets are located. You're likely to meet hunters in Waialae Canyon and you're likely to see evidence of their success by the bones and the carcases of animals left along the trail.

There is ample water in the canyon, but it should be treated, filtered or boiled before drinking.

Waimea Canyon Trail, 1.5 miles, 2 hours.
Trailhead is in Waimea Canyon.

You reach the trail by hiking down the Kukui Trail to the river, or by hiking seven miles up-river from Waimea town. The latter not only requires permission from a number of private parties but is a hot, exhausting trek. The Waimea Canyon Trail also provides access to the Koaie and Kaluahaulu trails and to the inner recesses of the canyon.

The Waimea Canyon Trail travels north from the end of the Kukui Trail through the canyon to the junction of Koaie Stream and Waimea River. Well-maintained, it leads up the river on the west side to a point where a plantation ditchman's house is located. The trail was originally constructed for access to the canyon to construct and maintain a powerhouse up-river.

There is ample water in the canyon, but it should be treated, filtered or boiled before drinking.

Wainininua Trail, .6 mile, 1/2 hour (hike rating: hardy family).
Park HQ to trailhead 2.2 miles.

Mostly a short, flat, scenic forest walk, the Wainininua Trail with the Kumuwela Trail completes a loop off the Kumuwela Road. There are a variety of native and introduced plants, the most notable being aromatic ginger with its lovely, light-yellow blossoms. Many local girls like to put a fresh ginger blossom in their hair, not only for its beauty but also for its fragrance.

KOKEE — Northwest

Alakai Swamp, 3.5 miles, 3 hours (hike rating: strenuous).
Park HQ to trailhead 3 miles.

Few will disagree that the Alakai (lit., "to lead") Swamp is the most interesting and exciting place on the island. For interest, there is the beautiful mokihana berry — Kauai's flower — and the native rain-forests; and for excitement, there is the swamp with its bogs, where a false step puts you knee-deep in mud and water. I recommend a lightweight, gore-tex or cloth hiking boot for this trail. You can bet on getting very wet and muddy.

The trail begins deceivingly easily off Mohihi (Camp 10) Road, which should be traversed by a four-wheeled vehicle because parts are steep and deeply rutted. (An alternative route is off the Pihea Trail — see below.) A forest-reserve marker identifies the trailhead while the trail follows an old pole line constructed during World War ll for Army communciations. The trail is in good condition (1988) and taped so that it is not difficult to follow unless a heavy cloud cover is present.

The first bog is near the one-mile marker. After the Alakai-Pihea Trail junction, bogs become more frequent, wetter and deeper until the 2 1/2-mile marker, from where it is all bog until trail's end. Your nose will be your guide to the mokihana (Pelea anisata) tree, which emits a strong anise odor. It is a small tree whose small berries are strung and worn in leis. Native to the islands, the mokihana berry is frequently twined with the maile vine to make a popular wedding lei. The maile (Alyxia olivaeformis) vine is common along the trail, with its tiny, glossy leaves and tiny, white flowers. Unlike the Mokihana tree, the maile vine must be cut or its bark stripped before its musky, woodsy scent or anise is noticed.

After the first two miles of ascending and descending a number of small, fern-laden gulches, the broad, flat expanse of the swamp lies before you. There is little chance of getting off the trail if you follow the poleline route, even though many of the poles have been cut down. You may have to loop here and there to avoid the wetter, deeper bogs. At the 2 3/4-mile marker you must make a left turn, leaving the poleline to follow white pipe markers. Be alert and cautious and you will find your way.

At Kilohana ("lookout point" or "superior") Lookout one has a magnificent view into Wainiha (lit., "unfriendly water") Valley, which extends from the

Alakai Swamp Trail (?)

sea to the base of Mt. Waialeale. Beyond Wainiha lies Hanalei (lit., "crescent bay") with its conspicuous wide, deep bay. It's an enchanting place to picnic, rest and reflect. If the cloud cover prevents a view, just wait and it is likely to clear.

Awaawapuhi Trail, 3.1 miles, 3 hours (hike rating: strenuous).
Park HQ to trailhead 1.5 miles.

The trail begins north of Highway 55 at telephone pole No. 1-4/2P/152, about halfway between the Kokee Museum and the Kalalau lookout. There is a forestry trail marker at the trailhead. The trail is well-maintained, and mileage markers show the way. In 1988, the Division of Forestry identified and posted with

Awaawapuhi Trailhead

white PVC pipe 58 plants found along the trail. The white pipe with numbers on top identify the plants while the pipes with numbers on the side are mile markers. The Division of Forestry has a guide "Awa'awa'puhi Botanical Trail Guide," which is available from the forestry office in Lihue (see Appendix). Learning about these native and introduced plants will add a dimension to your experience.

In 1988, the Hawaii State Division of Forestry completed cutting, brushing, posting and taping the Nualolo Trail and the Nualolo Cliff Trail (see map) so that a marvelous 9-mile hike is possible by following the Awaawapuhi-Cliff-Nualolo Trails. I would begin such a trek on the Nualolo Trail and end traversing the Awaawapuhi Trail since the latter is a more gradual ascent.

Of the trails that extend to points high above the Na Pali Coast and the extraordinarily beautiful valleys of the north shore, this is the best. You should be in good condition before attempting this hike and be prepared with water and food. The rewards are great as you pass through tropical forests to view the extremely precipitous and verdant valleys of Awaawapuhi (lit., "ginger valley") and Nualolo.

The first part of the trail and the trail passes through a moist native forest, dominated by koa trees, for a pleasant, cool hike. Koa trees grow to a height of more than 50 feet. The kos has a light gray bark that is smooth on young trees and considerably furrowed on mature trees. The leaves are smooth, stiff and crescent-shaped. Often called Hawaiian mahogany, the wood is red with wavy grain that makes it popular for use in furniture, woodwork and ukuleles. In older times it had nobler purposes, having been used for war canoes, surfboards and calabashes. A variety of ferns, the beautiful kahili ginger, and edible passion fruit,

thimbleberries, and blackberries are also found along
the trail.

The trail descends gradually through a moist native forest which becomes drier scrub as it reaches the
ridges above the valley. You are most likely to see
feral goats in the pali area. With binoculars you can
watch goats forage while you pause on any one of a
number of lookouts about 2500 feet above the valley.
Additionally, you will probably sight helicopters flying
tourists in, out, and over the pali, since the Na Pali
Coast is a favorite for those who are unable or unwill-
ing to make the trip on foot.

Just before reaching the 3-mile marker, a white
PVC-pipe post identifies the Cliff Trail that goes
northeast (left) 2.1-miles to the Naulolo Trail, which
leads to the main road between the ranger's house and
the housekeeping cabins.

The Awaawapuhi Trail continues for 0.3 mile
from the junction to a vertical perch above the Na Pali
Coast. This is the best place to lunch and to watch for
goats while enjoying enchanting views into Nualolo
and Awaawapuhi valleys. Its is a startling and exciting
place.

**Honopu Trail, 2.5 miles, 2 1/2 hours (hike rating:
strenuous).**
Park HQ to trailhead 2.0 miles.

Officially, this trail is CLOSED. There is no trailhead sign. The Division of Forestry prefers that hikers
take the Awaawapuhi Trail, which is their showpiece.
The Honopu Trail is not maintained, but is still used by
hunters. The District Forester says that the trail will be
cleaned and opened when funds become available.

The trail begins about 1/2-mile past the
Awaawapuhi trailhead north (left) off Highway 55
where the road turns and ascends after a steep down-

hill. Like the Nualolo and the Awaawapuhi trails, this one provides excellent points from which to view the Na Pali Coast. The Honopu (lit., "conch bay") Trail is not maintained and it is dangerous in places where slides make passage along the pali difficult. The trail snakes along a ridge through dry forested areas and then through scrub forests typical of the area. At numerous points you can look deep into Honopu Valley, the so-called "Valley of the Lost Tribe," where the remains of an ancient Polynesian village have created a mystery as to who were these people and what happened to them.

Luxury camping — Kokee State Park

Kawaikoi Stream Trail, 2.5 (loop) miles, 1-1/2 hours (hike rating: hardy family).
Park HQ to trailhead 3.8 miles.

Access to the Kawaikoi (lit., "the flowing water") Stream Trail is off the Mohihi (Camp 10) Road, which is passable only in a four-wheel-drive vehicle. A 2 1/2-mile loop trail hike was made possible in 1975 when the Forest Service and the Hawaii Chapter of the Sierra Club connected the Kawaikoi Trail with the Pihea Trail.

The route begins opposite a planted forest of Japanese sugi pines and follows the south side of Kawaikoi Stream along an easy, well-defined trail in heavy vegetation. During rainy periods, this is a muddy trail. A short distance past the 0.5-mile point, a trail sign indicates a place to cross the stream to join the Pihea Trail on the north side of the stream. If the rocks are not visible, then the water is too high for safe crossing. The Kawaikoi Trail itself continues east on the south side of the stream to a point 100 yards past the 3/4-mile marker, where a trail sign marks the loop portion of the trail. During the 1-mile loop it is necessary to cross the stream twice.

In recent years, there has been a good deal of grass planting and herbicide work in the area in an effort to control blackberry, which is threatening to take over not only this area but also a number of other areas in the park.

There are many swimming holes in this generous stream and places along the bank to spend some peaceful moments. You may agree with Ralph Daehler, District Forester, who has told me that Kawaikoi is the most beautiful place on Kauai.

Kohua Ridge Trail, 2.5 miles, 3 hours (hike rating: strenuous).

Park HQ to trailhead 5.5 miles.

The trailhead to the Kohua Ridge Trail (formerly the Maile Flat Trail) is off the Mohihi (Camp 10) Road, which is passable only in a four-wheel-drive vehicle. In 1988, the trail was cleaned and extended to Maile Flat for supurb views of Waimea Canyon.

Originally constructed by the Civilian Conservation Corps, the Kohua Ridge Trail is a vigorous hike up Kohua Ridge to Maile Flat, which contains a heavy undergrowth of maile (Alyxia olivaeformis). A fragrant vine, maile has glossy leaves, tiny white flowers and a musky, woodsy scent of anise when it is cut or its bark is stripped. Combined with mokihana berries, it is a popular lei for weddings.

From the trailhead, the trail crosses the Mohihi Stream and follows a steep and eroded path to the top of the ridge. It is a popular trail for goat hunters who continue beyond Maile Flat on an unmaintained trail.

Mohihi-Waiale Trail, 9 miles, overnight hike (hike rating: difficult).

Park HQ to trailhead 6.2 miles.

By 1988, the first three miles of this trail had been cleared. DO NOT hike beyond the cleared portion since the old trail is in disrepair as it cuts a circuitious route through the Alakai Swamp to Waialae Stream.

The trail begins at the end of the Mohihi (Camp 10) Road, crosses Mohihi Stream, skirts the upper part of the Koaie drainage, continues along a ridgetop to an intersection with the trail to Mt. Waialele in the Alakai Swamp, and them drops into Waialae Stream Valley to the Waialae Camp area. Camping is permitted both at the Koaie Stream rain guage and at the Waialae Camp Shelter.

Originally constucted by the Civilian Conservation Corps in the 1930's, the trail segment connecting
the Mohihi-Waialae Trail and the Waialae Canyon
Trail was destroyed by a hurricane in 1959. When
funds become available, the trail will be repaired
according to state officials.

Nualolo Trail, 3.8 miles, 3 hours, 1500 feet loss (hike rating: strenuous).
50 yards west of Park HQ.

In 1988, the Hawaii State Division of Forestry
completed cutting, brushing, posting, and taping the
Nualolo Trail and the Nualolo Cliff Trail so that a
marvelous 9-mile hike is possible by following the
Nualolo-Cliff-Awaawapuhi trails. The Nualolo Trail
starts between the ranger station and the housekeeping
cabins in Kokee, and if you follow the 9-mile hike
suggested above, you exit the Awaawapuhi Trail on
Highway 55, 1.5 miles from park headquarters. From
here it is easy to hitch a ride back to your car.

The first part of the trail passes through a native
forest of koa trees with their crescent-shaped leaves
for a pleasant, cool hike. After an initial ascent of
about 300 feet, the trail then descends about 1500 feet
to a number of viewpoints overlooking Nualolo Valley. In 1988, the trail was cleaned so that the first 1.5
miles are broad, posted and easy to follow. A variety
of ferns, the beautiful ahili ginger, and edible passion
fruit, thimbleberries and blackberries are found along
the trail.

The trail narrows somewhat at the 1.5-mile marker,
but then opens again at the 2.25-mile post. After this
point, you're certain to see the rare, endemic iliau
plant (see Black Pipe Trail for description). You may
also likely to find ripe strawberry guava, a small, red
golf ball-sized fruit.

Pali above Kalalau Valley

There are several steep parts on the trail in the last mile so be cautious. At the 3.4-mile marker, the Cliff Trail goes right for 2.1 miles until it reaches the Awaawapuhi Trail and the Nualolo Trail goes straight to numerous vista points about 2800 feet above the valley. It is a marvelous place to picnic and to enjoy the solitude. If you walk out to the end of the ridge, you will have a view of the Na Pali Coast to the north (right). You can see the beach in Kalalau Valley.

Nualolo Cliff Trail, 2.1 miles, 1 1/2 hours, (hike rating: hardy family).
Reached via Nualolo or Awaawapuhi Trail.

If you have reached the Nualolo Cliff Trail junction from the Awaawapuhi or Nualolo Trail, you should take the Cliff Trail for the views into Awaawapuhi and Naulolo valleys are outstanding. Additionally, you're likely to see feral goats here as well as the rare, delicately beautiful Kauai hibiscus.

From the Nualolo Trail, the Nualolo Cliff Trail is mostly level until just before reaching the Awaawapuhi Trail, where it makes an easy ascent. One-fourth-mile markers identify the way along which you are certain to see goats foraging for food and bounding on the steep slopes in the upper valley. In 1988, the trail was cut to provide hikers with a crossover trail between two marvelous trails and to offer some of the best views of the Na Pali Coast.

At the 1.5-mile point, the trail emerges on a flat area used by campers. Here, the trail is not clearly marked. Hike up the ridge away from the valley lookout and you will locate the trail and shortly, a white PVC-pipe-marker.

Between the 0.5 and 0.25-mile markers, look for the rare, endemic Kauai hibiscus (Saint johnianus) with its small, delicate, orange blossom. It's a find.

After an easy uphill, the Naulolo Cliff Trail joins the Awaawapuhi Trail where you can go 0.3 miles left to the end of the trail or go 2.8 miles right to Kokee Road.

Pihea Trail, 3.75 miles, 3 hours (hike rating: strenuous).
Park HQ to trailhead 3.8 miles.

Pihea ("din of voices crying, shouting, wailing, lamentaion") Trail begins at the end of the Highway 55 at Puu o Kila (lit., "Kila's Hill") overlooking Kalalau Valley. A hiking trail registery identifies the trailhead.

The first 3/4 mile follows the remains of a county road project which was begun in a cloud of controversy and which terminated literally in the mire when money ran out, along with the willingness to continue. A road through the Alakai Swamp and down the mountain to Hanalei would have been a great tourist attraction and an engineering feat, but an ecological disaster.

From the lookout, you can usually see the white-tailed tropic bird (Phaethon lepturus) soaring along the cliffs of Kalalau Valley. This bird is white with large black wing patches above and 16-inch tail streamers. A similar bird that is all white except for red tail streamers is the red-tailed tropic bird (Phaethon rubricauda).

After enjoying the breathtaking views into Kalalau, your trail follows the rim of the valley to Pihea, the last overlook into Kalalau before the Alakai Swamp. The trail makes an abrupt right turn as it enters the swamp and then drops in and out of a number of gulches to the junction with the Alakai Swamp Trail.

The Pihea Trail can be used as part of a loop trip from Kalalau into the Alakai Swamp, with a return to park headquarters via the Alakai Swamp Trail or the Kawaikoi Stream Trail and the Camp 10 Road.

Both the maile vine and the mokihana tree (see the Alakai Swamp Trail for description) are common along the trail and are favorites of both locals and visitors. The mokihana's powerful anise aroma attracts immediate attention.

Also common in this area is the ohia lehua (Metrosideros polymorpha), with its tufted red stamens that remind the visitor of the bottlebrush tree. A variety of tree ferns abound along the trail, the hapu'u (Cibotium chamissoi) and the amaumau (Sadleria cyatheoides) being most common. The latter grows to 10 feet. Its pinnate fronds were once used for huts and the juice from it for a reddish dye.

From the junction with the Alakai Swamp Trail, our trail continues over the newest portion passing through native forests, crossing small streams, and winding through verdant gulches until it joins the Kawaikoi Stream Trail.

Poomau Canyon, .3 mile, 15 minutes (hike rating: hardy family).
Park HQ to trailhead 4.5 miles.

About 0.5 mile past the trailhead for the Kawaikoi Stream Trail on the Mohihi (Camp 10) Road is a marker identifying the Poomau (lit., "constant source") Canyon Trail. This short, easy trail passes through a small stand of Japanese sugi trees, enters a native rainforest, and ends overlooking Poomau Canyon, the largest and northernmost side canyon in Waimea Canyon. Across the canyon on the west rim, the high prominence is Puu Ka Pele (lit., "Pele's Hill") and Highway 55. Legend records that Pele, the fire goddess, left Kauai unable to find a suitable home. The caldera was created when Pele brought down her foot for the leap across the channel to Oahu. The caldera has since been filled with small stones by visitors as an offering to the goddess — or so some say. The lookout is an excellent place for pictures of the canyon and for picnicking.

Waialeale Wilderness Trail
Mt. Waialeale is the highest place (5,208 at Kawaikini Peak) on Kauai and the wettest place on the face of the earth, with an annual rainfall between 400 and 600 inches! It also has religious significance for many Hawaiians, with seven of the most sacred heiaus — pre-Christian places of worship — extending from the shore to the summit.

There is no existing trail to the summit and there are no plans to construct one. Ralph Daehler, District Forester for Kauai, states that hiking is discouraged in the Waialeale portion of the Alakai Swamp because of the danger and of the fragile nature of the area. It is closed to hiking until such time as trails are established and rules and regulations for their use defined. He noted that Waialeale is an important watershed area and has to be protected.

Kalalau Lookout — what a sight!

Appendix

Division of State Parks
State Building
3060 Eiwa St, Room 306
Lihue, HI. 96766
808/245-4444

1. Camping permits for state parks and Kalalau Trail.
2. Hiking information.

Division of Forestry
State Building
3060 Eiwa St, Room 306
Lihue, HI. 96766
808/245-4433

1. Hiking information.

Kokee Lodge
P.O. Box 819
Waimea, HI 96796
808/335-6061

1. Kokee cabin information and reservations.

Department of Parks
and Recreation
County of Kauai
4280A Rice St. Bldg.B
Lihue, HI. 96766
808/245-1881

1. Camping permits for county parks (reservations by mail, but permits must be picked up in person).

Hanalei Camping &
Backpacking Inc.
Ching Young Village
P.O. Box 1245
Hanalei, HI. 96714
808/826-6664

1. Complete line of camping and backpacking equipment; sales and rentals. (New store in Kekaha to serve Kokee/Waimea area)

Index

ORDER FORM

HIKING KAUAI $7.95

Forward to: _____

Name: _____

Address: _____

City: _____ State: _____ Zip: _____

Quantity   Price   Total
                          @ $7.95

              CA residents add $.48 tax
                  per book ordered =

                Shipping/Handling
                   (Book rate) = $1.00

        I'm adding another buck,
           so send it 1st class =
                                    _____

        TOTAL ENCLOSED: =
                                    _____
                                    _____

MAIL TO:
Hawaiian Outdoor Adventures
P. O. Box 30697
Long Beach, CA 90853